Praise for *Miracles at Work*

"*Miracles at Work* shows you how to take the wisdom and inspiration of *A Course of Miracles* to work with you every day. It helps transform the world of work from labor to love, competition to grace, and chronic busyness to meaningful success. Thank you, Emily!"

ROBERT HOLDEN
author of *Authentic Success* and *Holy Shift! 365 Daily Meditations from A Course in Miracles*

"We all know that 'love' is the center of spiritual tradition, but it's not always clear how to apply it on the job. This book is a gem of insight into both the principles of the *Course* as well as practical ways to bring them to work each day."

CHRISTINE HASSLER
author of *Expectation Hangover*

"Emily Bennington has written a beautiful and deeply practical book that has the power to completely reframe the way you think about work and business. If you apply the lessons in this book, which Emily elucidates with precision and obvious affection for *A Course in Miracles*, you will experience not only inner shifts, but tangible outer shifts as well."

JORDAN BACH
life coach

"Emily is a glowing, bright light for the business world. She beautifully breaks down the principles of *A Course in Miracles* and explains them in such an accessible, practical way that you can immediately start to integrate them into your work life. This book is going to be a game-changer for anyone from a college graduate just entering the workforce to a seasoned CEO ready for more ease, flow, and abundance."

CASSANDRA BODZAK
author and host of Eat with Intention TV

"There aren't many books that are as practical as they are aligned with spiritual knowing. *Miracles at Work* delivers both in a straightforward, witty, and warm way."

ROBYN YOUKILIS
author of *Go with Your Gut*

"Emily astutely interprets the *Course* for a business and leadership audience, providing a pathway for those of us who want to succeed to also be unapologetic about our hunger to be spiritual. And she's funny. So funny. How refreshing to have a bold voice in the self-improvement space who is as witty as she is whip-smart."

ALEXIA VERNON
creator of Influencer Academy and Your Spotlight Talk

"Happiness and transformation are available during business hours. With brilliant simplicity and relatable workplace examples, *Miracles at Work* will guide you to embody the inner peace that is available to all of us, regardless of workplace demands, and to be the colleague and leader whose presence truly inspires others."

CORINNE ZUPKO
EdS, author and corporate mindfulness teacher

"Emily has combined the profound wisdom of *A Course in Miracles* with the practical insights of the business world to create this economic survival manual for the twenty-first century—with spiritual dividends."

BEVERLY HUTCHINSON MCNEFF
founder and president of Miracle Distribution Center

"I found this book to be simple enough to follow even for the beginning ACIM student, but deep enough in its principles and practices to appeal to the most advanced. As a 20-year student of the *Course* myself, I would not have thought it could be done. Thank you, Emily, for giving us this much-needed guide for bringing spirituality into the workplace. An extraordinary work!"

BARBARA GOODMAN SIEGEL
OMC, author, career coach, and spiritual counselor

MIRACLES AT WORK

Other Works by Emily Bennington

Who Says It's a Man's World: The Girls' Guide to Corporate Domination

Effective Immediately: How to Fit In, Stand Out, and Move Up at Your First Real Job

Turning
Inner Guidance
Into Outer Influence

MIRACLES AT WORK

EMILY BENNINGTON

BOULDER, COLORADO

Sounds True
Boulder, CO 80306

Published 2017

Cover design by Jennifer Miles
Book design by Beth Skelley

Printed in Canada

Library of Congress Cataloging-in-Publication Data
Names: Bennington, Emily, author.
Title: Miracles at work : turning inner guidance into outer influence / Emily Bennington.
Description: Boulder, Colorado : Sounds True, 2017.
Identifiers: LCCN 2016028258 (print) | LCCN 2016047548 (ebook) | ISBN 9781622037247 (pbk.) | ISBN 9781622037254 (ebook)
Subjects: LCSH: Course in Miracles. | Work—Religious aspects. | Job satisfaction—Religious aspects. | Career development. | Spirituality.
Classification: LCC BL65.W67 B465 2017 (print) | LCC BL65.W67 (ebook) | DDC 650.1—dc23
LC record available at https://lccn.loc.gov/2016028258

10 9 8 7 6 5 4 3 2 1

To Helen Schucman and William Thetford for bringing
A Course in Miracles into the world.

And to my grandmother, Mary Lou Bennington,
who didn't need it to embody unconditional love.

There is a light in you the world can not perceive.
And with its eyes you will not see this light,
for you are blinded by the world.
Yet you have eyes to see it.

A COURSE IN MIRACLES **(W-PI.189.1:1–3)**

CONTENTS

Foreword

BY MARIANNE WILLIAMSON

Knowledge is power. And there is no greater power than spiritual insight because it is the deepest knowledge of all. It is the understanding of who we are and how we operate, how we fit into the universe, and where our true power lies.

In *Miracles at Work*, Emily Bennington applies her understanding of one of the greatest spiritual teachings of our time or of any time, *A Course in Miracles*, to an area of great importance and at times great anxiety for millions of people. The idea of "taking the bull by the horns" has turned out to be a questionable prescription for professional success; while it sometimes promotes success and sometimes does not, it also causes frequent suffering to us and to those around us. High stress, anxiety, lack of peace of mind, and broken relationships frequently litter our career paths as we struggle day in and day out to handle the normal complications of professional life. Something is desperately wrong when there are so many headaches and heartaches among those who are struggling to make it in the world.

Yet is there an alternative? It's not enough to simply detach from a dysfunctional worldview; our need is to embrace a better one. *A Course in Miracles* is a better one, and Bennington teaches it beautifully. She guides us beyond the entrenched paradigm that dominates our current thinking about career, beginning, to quote *A Course in Miracles*, by "considering the possibility that there might be a better way." We can switch our mental filter from one that promotes an endless cascade of anxiety to one that promotes inner peace.

Only when the psyche is transformed from an instrument of chaos to an instrument of love are our circumstances transformed from pain to peace. Our work lives can change only when we change.

The spiritual journey is a path of the heart, an internal process with external effects. Fundamental spiritual changes—from thoughts of blame to thoughts of blessing, and thoughts of condemnation to thoughts of forgiveness—affect every area of our lives because they change *us*. They lift us above the harsh and anxious energies that block our good by blocking our relationships and undermining our skills. As Bennington writes, "Love cannot transform your career until it transforms you first."

Mainstream understanding of spirituality has changed over the last few decades. It is no longer seen as a category separate from the rest of our existence, but rather a template for right living that underlies them all. Love is no longer seen as just some soft, gooey thing to be relegated to only some aspects of life, but rather the meaning and essence of life itself. The path of the heart is relevant to everything.

Learning the practical application of that principle, however, is not always easy—especially in the workplace. Many would question what it actually means to bring love into the conference room. Thus the importance of this book.

Using the principles of *A Course in Miracles* to guide the reader through everyday work situations any modern professional can relate to, Bennington articulates a path out of hell for the harried, stressed-out employer or employee. As we switch from primary identification with our worldly roles to identification with our spiritual function as practitioners of love and forgiveness, we don't find ourselves less effective at work; rather, the opposite. We find ourselves calmer, more peaceful, and more appreciated by others. Spirituality is not a life of sacrifice; it is a life of greater power both within and without.

Bennington is not naïve about the modern work world. As someone who has counseled numerous executives and has written bestselling books on career success, she knows whereof she speaks about worldly as well as spiritual matters. She knows that bringing the two into right alignment is a recipe for success both personally and professionally, and by writing this book she has done a great service for anyone seeking a more peaceful, more successful life. In Bennington's words, "Spiritual intelligence becomes far more than just a tool for professional growth: it becomes a fundamental change in your entire worldview."

This book, then, will not only offer you guidance for the workplace; it will offer you guidance for your entire life. As you read it, you will begin to repair the thought that there was ever a separation between the two. It is sometimes very hard to "find the love" when trying to make deadlines, work the numbers, and pay the bills. But Bennington makes the important point that the only way to "find the love" is to *be* the love, wherever we are and whatever we're doing.

Such is the miracle. Such is the work. Such is this book.

Introduction

IS BUSINESS SPIRITUAL?

"Okay, everyone, put down your Starbucks and close your eyes."

The conference director appeared nervous and slightly overwhelmed as he stood at the podium and looked into the crowd of CEOs, educators, and entrepreneurs who had gathered in Washington, DC, for a mindful leadership summit.

Actually, he seemed rather surprised we'd shown up.

Could a group of hyper-ambitious, logic-driven executives *really* be interested in a twenty-six-hundred-year-old contemplative practice?

And yet, there we were.

More than five hundred strong, all jammed into a gallery space so tight that people were lucky even to stand in the back. (Unlucky ones had to watch via streaming video next door.)

TIIIIIIIIIIIINNNNNNNNGGGGG . . .

The opening chime echoed loudly around the room as the roar of hundreds of conversations occurring all at once began to settle and then . . . silence.

This was not our first rodeo.

"Thank you," said the director. "Now, for just a moment I'd like you to think about what brought you here. I'd like you to think about what you hope to achie—"

He didn't have to finish the sentence.

I already knew.

In fact, I had come to DC for the sole purpose of asking a question that had been tormenting me ever since my career-coaching business began to attract clients whose challenges went far beyond work.

Betrayal.

Addiction.

Cancer diagnosis.
Loss of a child.
Resurfacing childhood trauma.
Believe me, I could go on.

As each story became more complex, there was something I deeply wanted to share with these clients—and yet I always held back. Eventually, the idea of *not* sharing it would start to bother me again and the whole cycle would begin anew.

By attending the summit, I had come to consult my tribe. After all, these were executives with meditation rooms next to boardrooms. The ones who wear mala beads with business suits and vacation at ashrams. If anyone would understand my struggle, surely I was looking at them.

This is how I found myself holding a microphone in front of the entire audience and a panel of gurus, finally asking the question that had been spinning in my head for almost two years:

"If mindfulness is a spiritual practice at its roots, then what role does spirituality play in business and leadership?"

There was a loud sigh from somewhere in the crowd behind me and a moment of awkward silence when members of the panel looked at each other as if to say,

"You take it."

"No, you take it."

"No, *you* take it."

Before anyone could answer, however, the moderator stepped in and gave a response that basically went like this:

Business isn't spiritual. Next question, please.

Afterward, a few people pulled me aside to reinforce the message, one of whom memorably remarked that "God is like porn. You only do it when you have to, in private, and you *never* talk about it."

For a while I listened to this advice and tried to separate my "spiritual" work from my "real" work in careers—but it never stuck. Before long the same old questions would come knocking again, growing louder every time.

How can we capably lead ourselves and our teams during times of intense challenge without the shifts in perspective that spirituality provides?

How can we bring these shifts into our jobs every day without colleagues thinking we're naïve, unfollowable, or otherwise unpromotable?

It's interesting to note that, as of this writing, the most recent Pew Research survey on religious trends found that roughly 84 percent of the global population identifies with a particular tradition of faith.[1] Moreover, even among the 16 percent who claim to have no religious affiliation at all, many still retain what are considered to be spiritual convictions—belief in an immortal soul, for example. As such, when you consider the fact that the vast majority of the world seems to have some form of spiritual grounding, and when you combine that with the fact that full-time professionals work an average of forty hours each week (and often many more) *is it any wonder that the line between work and spirituality would be a little blurry*?

We consistently spend more time on the job than we do with our families (or doing anything else for that matter—including sleeping[2]) and yet any influence our spiritual life could have on our career is expected to be checked at the door each day.

Not surprisingly, this isn't working for thousands of professionals facing personal challenges similar to the ones described earlier. It's also not working for those who simply want to parlay the best lessons of faith—for example, humility, compassion, and nonattachment—into their jobs without fear of being judged as weak, off-putting, or unsophisticated.

Sound familiar? If so, then you're in the right place. With this book, my goal is not only to show you that spiritual principles *do* have a role to play at all levels of business, but also to show you how the path of a metaphysical text called *A Course in Miracles*, in particular, is a secret to leadership itself.

I know because, as both a longtime student of the *Course* and a mindful leadership coach to professionals around the world, I've seen these results first hand. In my own career, to say that the *Course* has been a benefit would be a massive understatement.

It transformed everything.

Simply put, the more I kept coming back to this mysterious blue book, the more I started to experience the remarkable perspective shifts it promised. On the outside, nothing had really "changed" per se—I still had the same job, the same drive, and the same deadlines as before—but the inner transformations were undeniable.

The critical voice disappeared.

The white-knuckle grip on outcomes vanished.

A "crisis" could no longer derail my whole day.

Most of all, my relationships improved **dramatically**.

These are the results I want for you too, and by applying the principles of *A Course in Miracles* via the lessons and exercises in this book, I know that your career will undergo many similarly remarkable and lasting transformations:

- You will exhibit the kind of leadership presence that colleagues and supervisors can't help but notice—and want to follow.

- Your frustration level with workplace challenges and obstacles will decrease as your perspective undergoes a profound shift.

- The emotional charge you feel around difficult work relationships will diminish—and you'll know what to do when it arises again.

- You will work more effectively in teams and find more joy in the experience.

- You will make better, more clear-eyed decisions.

- Your entire professional experience will be infused with a sense of grace and ease.

The most succinct way to summarize the *Course*'s impact on your career is to say that when you are no longer available for chaotic thinking, the chaos in your life falls away. While the *effects* of these perspective shifts are external and will become visible to your colleagues instantly, as you'll discover, the *cause* of these transformations is very much internal—and very much spiritual.

To be clear, however, given the level of suspicion that can—and should—accompany any particular religion seeking to encroach into business, your colleagues (and my fellow summit attendees) will be pleased to know that this is NOT a book about proclaiming your faith or recruiting new *Course* students in the office.

In fact, let me state my opinion around this up front: please don't.

Rather, this is a book about Love applied to work. But not romantic love, naïve love, or even boundaryless love. Like the *Course* itself, this is about a sacred Love for all life. It's a *holy* Love that goes beyond any form of behavior or personality difference to the very core of our interbeing. The ancient Greeks called this love *agape.* In Eastern traditions, the spirit of this love has been compared to a bird with two wings—wisdom and compassion—that each need the other to fly. Given this reframe, how could the world *not* benefit from an infusion of spirituality at work?

This is what makes the *Course* such a remarkable career path. Not because it defines God as Love (which it does, but that would hardly make it unique). What makes the *Course* unique is that it shows you how to radically improve your life by applying this same sacred Love to everything, including—and for our purposes, *especially*—your job. As you already know, if life is a classroom, then work is definitely where we get some of our trickiest assignments. And so the question we'll answer together is how you can show up for these assignments as your highest Self.

Sounds simple, but it's not. The complexities of business today, especially when paired with personality differences and the speed at which we are challenged to move, make life at work profoundly difficult.

And yet, as you begin to bring forth the kinds of miracles the *Course* teaches, get ready, because the people who have been waiting for a new business culture to emerge have been waiting for you. Proselytizing won't inspire them, *but your authentic presence will.* This is because the Love that soars through a mind connected to both wisdom and compassion will always demonstrate the truest of all spiritual truths: grace, not rank, is our real power.

By contrast, a career on the wings of judgment and competition simply cannot fly.

Actually, as I was writing this book, I was frequently reminded that workplace dysfunction was one of the factors that caused the *Course* to be written in the first place. I'll let you read the story of how it came to be in the FAQs in the appendix, but suffice it to say that more than fifty years ago the scribes of the *Course* used their own office challenges as a catalyst to create a masterpiece—and a movement—that continues to inspire millions around the world to this day.

Indeed, business really is spiritual after all.

Welcome to miracles at work.

Emily

A NOTE ON THE PHILOSOPHY AND STRUCTURE OF THIS BOOK

Spiritual or religious?

Before we begin, I think it would be useful to share some thoughts on how this book is organized. First and foremost, I'd like to point out that this is a spiritual book and not a religious one. While much parsing can been done between these two words, I tend to subscribe to the broad view that religion entails an organized and specific set of beliefs and rituals, while spirituality reflects the innate need we all have to connect to something greater and more intelligent than ourselves. This does not make religion and spirituality opposites, only different roads that lead to the same place. We can recognize and honor our unique paths for their role in shaping our sense of culture and identity, while also knowing that the path is not the destination. It is merely one way to get there.

That said, this is a book that talks about God. From the very first chapter we dive very deep, very fast, and I do not want to sugarcoat or tread lightly around this. Therefore, consider yourself warned that we will go all in. It is my belief that the principles within *A Course in Miracles* have the ability to transform your entire career experience—regardless of your position or industry—and to accurately convey the *Course*'s principles, I've chosen to keep the *Course*'s language. This includes using traditionally Christian words like "God," "Christ," and "Holy Spirit," although you'll discover the *Course* uses these words in decidedly nontraditional ways. (Please see the FAQs section in the back of this book for more on this topic.)

Even so, you are not being asked to give up any of your existing affiliations or traditions here, nor are you being asked to adopt any new ones. The goal is simply to use the principles of *A Course in Miracles* to connect to an experience of transcendent wisdom and compassion (i.e., Love), which has the added benefit of elevating your professionalism and leadership ability at work. Whether you are currently on a spiritual path or not, my hope is that you will find that these tools integrate into your journey, while enhancing it at the same time.

Love vs. love

As you read this book you'll notice that sometimes Love will appear capitalized and other times it won't (love). This is not the result of sloppy editing. It is the result of an attempt to provide some context regarding when the love being referenced is spiritual (Love) and when it's the product of our own emotion (love). Unfortunately, the word "love" in the English language already does a fair amount of acrobatics as we bend it one way to describe transient things ("I love this song!") and another way to describe our most sacred bonds ("I love my family.") I'm afraid I have made it work even harder to incorporate a spiritual interpretation, so please be mindful of the context whenever you see L/love as we go along. (Note: This principle also applies to other words you will find capitalized here and in the *Course* as well. For example, "self" refers to the body while "Higher Self" refers to spirit, and so on.)

How this book is organized

I have divided *Miracles at Work* into two parts: part one, "Fire Your self," and part two, "Hire Your Self." In part one, we cover what it means to let go of your "self" (little "s"), which you'll soon discover is the primary block to the presence of wisdom and compassion in business. Indeed, according to the *Course*, a major impediment to success—professional and otherwise—is the mistaken belief that we are all separate "selves" in individual bodies, drifting on our own without any real connection or support. This, you'll learn, could not be further from the Truth. The *Course* teaches that the small self is merely an illusion, created and maintained by what it calls the "ego," and designed to keep us mired in fear-based thinking and a long trail of broken relationships. Thus, the first half of this book is structured to help you recognize those moments when the ego is, quite literally, *at work* and thereby impeding your experience of a joyful, fulfilling career.

With the ego unmasked, in part two, "Hire Your Self," you'll discover how to create miracles in earnest. Specifically, this section dives into how to shift your thinking in a way that aligns with greater influence and leadership presence, while maintaining a sense of deep, abiding peace. You will learn how to recognize and connect with your inner guidance, why every encounter has the potential to be sacred, and what it really means to allow the presence of Love to "work" through you. This, says the *Course*, is not only your function, but it is also the key to your joy and, as we'll cover, your influence. As the best leaders have demonstrated, there is no such thing as "finding" or "achieving" success that is sustainable over time. You *attract* success based on who you are and the values and character you bring to each interaction you have. And since you cannot lead or motivate others with the Real you if you don't know who that is, the second half of this book will take you on what the *Course* calls the "journey without distance" (T-8.VI.9:7), where you will be given the tools to accept the Magnitude that is your natural inheritance. By the end of this section, you will understand how one concept within the *Course* builds upon the other until the definition of a "miracle at work" is fully formed and seen from all angles. I know you will be delighted, as am I, by how beautifully and elegantly *Course* teachings reinforce one another, not to mention how deeply they inspire.

Exercises and *Course* references

At the end of each chapter you will find a series of reflection exercises called Course Work, which are designed to help you implement key concepts right away. You don't have to own a copy of *A Course in Miracles* to benefit from these exercises, but it is highly recommended because some of the work refers to specific passages for further reading.

In addition, throughout the book—and particularly in sections labeled Key Quotes—I've pulled excerpts from the *Course* related to the material being covered. These quotes include a numbering system that references where they can be found in the version of *A Course in Miracles* used for this writing (Foundation for Inner Peace, third edition). Examples of how to read this numbering system follow:

> Text-Chapter.Section.Paragraph:Sentence, e.g., T-3.IV.7:10
>
> Workbook-part.Lesson.Paragraph:Sentence, e.g., W-pI.169.5:2
>
> Manual-Question.Paragraph:Sentence, e.g., M-13.3:2
>
> Clarification of Terms-Section.Paragraph:Sentence, e.g., C-6.4:6
>
> Song of Prayer-Chapter.Section.Paragraph:Sentence, e.g., S-2.III:1:1

My deepest gratitude to the Foundation for Inner Peace for the permission to use these passages.

A final note on patience

Bringing spirituality into your life is a rewarding endeavor, albeit an often challenging one with many on-and-off moments along the way. Please be patient with yourself and know that when you incorporate what you are learning from the *Course* into your career, even "small" progress is big. There is no need to understand all of the concepts we discuss in these pages or in the *Course* right away—the only thing you need to understand at this point is that no moment you spend attempting to do so is wasted. *Every* step of your spiritual journey, no matter how tiny it may seem, contains the promise of transformation because every step gives you the opportunity to see that you are not walking alone.

For companion bonuses designed to enhance your *Course* and career journey, please visit miraclesatworkbook.com.

Part One

FIRE YOUR sELF

Whatever is true is eternal,
and cannot change or be changed.
Spirit is therefore unalterable because
it is already perfect, but the mind
can elect what it chooses to serve.

(T-1.V.5:1–2)

You have not only been fully created, but you have also been created perfect. There is no emptiness in you.

(T-2.I.1:3–4)

PERFECTION IS NOT A MATTER OF DEGREE

When my first son was eighteen months old we had him tested for autism. He was slow on motor skills, had troubling sensory issues, and despite the fact that his playmates were already stringing together basic sentences, the only word he could muster was "*Hi.*" It was literally all he would say, over and over again, all day long.

"Hi."

"Hi."

"Hi."

Out of answers, eventually our pediatrician sent us to a psychologist who ran a number of tests.

Does he accept help solving puzzles?

Can he transition to new activities without clinging to the old ones?

Does he get overly upset if his toys are taken away?

There are few things more distressing than waiting helplessly on the sidelines for a diagnosis of your child. And yet, after weeks of worrying, we were told that our son was going to be fine.

"He appears interested in developing relationships," said the psychologist. "Children with autism struggle with interpersonal skills, and in extreme cases they fail to see the difference between a person and an object like a chair."

As a career coach, this struck me as somewhat ironic since it rather fittingly described the majority of my clients' issues at work. While I was obviously relieved that the appointment went well, I admit I left that day thinking about what a fascinating experiment it would be to give professionals the same kind of test in the workplace that my son had just received in this doctor's office.

How do we collaborate on puzzles?

How do we transition to new experiences without clinging to old ones?

How do we react when our "toys" are taken away?

It's strange that the absence of meaningful interaction is considered a medical condition in children but often viewed as a strength in adults. If you've ever been treated by a boss or coworker with no more consideration than the average office chair, then you know exactly what I'm talking about here. To succeed in business requires the kind of "thick skin" and "resolve" that can often come across as emotionally neutered and yet anything less, we are told, is "soft."

What's worse is that we actually believe it.

This has led to work cultures where colleagues have a tendency to view each other less as human beings and more as objects along the path to a goal. Thankfully, there has been a valiant effort to right the ship with the relatively new field of emotional intelligence—an awareness of when feelings are driving behavior versus reason—and yet EQ (as it's often called) isn't the whole story. While there's no question that EQ is required to form long-term harmonious relationships in all aspects of life including work, there *is* another form of intelligence that is just as valuable and yet not nearly as well-known, namely *spiritual* intelligence or SQ.

If the idea of spiritual intelligence is new to you, SQ pioneer Cindy Wigglesworth describes it fittingly as "*the ability to behave with wisdom and compassion, while maintaining inner and outer peace, regardless of the situation.*"[1] Throughout this book we will be exploring what it means to bring SQ to work via the extraordinary lessons of *A Course in Miracles*, but first I'd like to zoom out and offer some context for why spiritual intelligence matters within a business setting at all.

Enter Stephen Covey

Like millions of professionals around the world, you may be familiar with author Stephen Covey as a result of his most popular book, *The 7 Habits of Highly Effective People*. While Covey was obviously not the first or the only person to develop a structured path to career success or emotional maturity, his work is uniquely important for our purposes because he succinctly describes it as leading from *dependence* (relying on others to meet our needs) to *independence* (taking responsibility for meeting our own needs) to *interdependence* (collaborating to resolve mutual needs). Because Covey and many others have written much on these subjects, I won't go into more detail here except to say that EQ is precisely what lays the groundwork for SQ.

In other words, the *emotionally intelligent* journey from dependence to interdependence is needed to begin the *spiritually intelligent* journey from interdependence to *interbeing*.

What this means is that the ability to understand the complex role of emotion within yourself and others is the *first* step, but the ultimate foundation of sacred Love is the ability to see no separation between yourself and others. As you'd expect, this is where traditional career advice forks and we find ourselves off-roading into an area where most business books refuse to go.

Spirituality. Religion. Metaphysics.

Call it what you want, but since we're here, let's begin with a basic question.

What is God?

Clearly that question is not so basic, but since it forms the ground of our journey through the *Course*, it seems like a worthy starting point.

In the Bible, when God was asked, "Who are you?" the response was said to be, "I AM."

> **You shall say to the sons of Israel, "I AM has sent me to you."**
>
> **(EXODUS 3:14)**

But what does *I AM* mean, anyway?

Does it mean that God is outside of us looking down (a spiritual tenet known as dualism), or does it mean that God is neither inside nor outside but everywhere (a.k.a. *non*dualism)?

To be clear, *A Course in Miracles* is very much a nondualistic text. In other words, a core part of its theology is that God doesn't perceive *anything* separate from Himself because *there is no "Himself."* As I mention in the *Course* FAQs located at the end of this book, God is genderless and beyond human form, so to say "Himself" isn't accurate anyway. But more than that, for God to "perceive Himself" *in relation* to something else is impossible if God is everything.

God is not partial.

(T-1.V.3:2)

Therefore, from a *Course* perspective it's not about whether God is outside or inside because there's no "you" reading this while "God" hovers in the ethers. There's just *God*—period—and you are in the mind of God.

This is the literal meaning of "I AM" and it's also what the introduction to the *Course* is referring to when it says, ". . . *what is all-encompassing can have no opposite.*"

How can something be opposite of all there is?

To take this a step further, if you look around the room right now, you may be wondering how it's possible for God to be both *everywhere* and *absolutely nowhere* at the same time. This, of course, brings us back to the original question: What is God? Is God an energy? A person? A force? All of the above?

The New Testament of the Bible provides an answer that simply says: "God is love" (John 4:8). The *Course* says the same thing, albeit with one glaring caveat. The *Course* describes God as *unconditional* love and goes on to say that *nothing else exists*. As the introduction to the *Course* states:

This course can therefore be summed up very simply in this way:

Nothing real can be threatened.
Nothing unreal exists.
Herein lies the peace of God.

(*COURSE* INTRODUCTION)

So to recap:

> God *is*.
> The *is* is Love.
> Love is *all* there is.

Let's stop here for a moment and consider how this relates to your career. Essentially, if you shift your definition of God from "a divine being looking down in judgment from the sky" to "the universal, formless energy of Love found in all life," *then this should shift how you define yourself as well.* "All life" includes you too, right? Accordingly, the journey of *A Course in Miracles* is the journey of recognizing that you not only *share* perfect Love, but that you ARE perfect Love along with everyone else.

Spirit is in a state of grace forever.
Your reality is only spirit.
Therefore you are in a state of grace forever.

(T-1.III.5:4–6)

Once you fully understand this, it becomes impossible to approach your job the same way ever again. As an example, "Russell from operations" is no longer just that guy down the hall with the personality that triggers you to no end. The shift from interdependence to interbeing is the shift from knowing that Russell *works* with you to knowing that he *is* you, which means you no longer view his welfare as separate from your own. This isn't something you do to be kind or altruistic, by the way. It's a perspective that naturally arises when your SQ grows to the point where you *know* that Love is present in both of you beyond what your eyes can see. Moreover, until you see this Love in him, the *Course* says, *you will not be able to see it in yourself.*

This is what makes spiritual intelligence such a superpower in the office. Just imagine the sense of calm and composure you could bring to your job, and the influence you would garner as a result, if you had the ability rise above all levels of human difference and disagreement simply by acknowledging the "reality of spirit" we share—*before* taking action.

Clearly, you don't need to voice this perception with anyone else at work and, again, you don't even need to call the Spirit we're describing here "God." You can call it "love," "light," or "human dignity," or you could use the Buddha's language: "inner luminosity." From a *Course* perspective, what matters isn't the language you use, but that you see this Spirit in all and that you know it is perfectly whole in all. As it says in the text:

. . . perfection is not a matter of degree.

(T-2.II.5:7)

This is the first principle you must understand if you want to get the most out of what the *Course* has to teach you: perfect in *one* means perfect in *all*. In other words, the Love in you and everyone else—the spiritual state of grace—cannot be flawed in some while flawless in others. Hence, Love cannot be earned through any specific religious practice or affiliation, nor does it shrink or expand based on what you do or don't do. Perfect doesn't mean *kind of* perfect. Perfect means perfect.

The problem, of course, is that spiritual perfection is totally invisible to us without our SQ superpowers. What this means is that, unless we intentionally sharpen up these skills, we'll continually go through life seeing only what our eyes tell us is true and missing the *truer* truth underneath. Worse, we won't even know we should be looking for it. Accordingly, this is what the *Course* means when it says, "*Let me recognize the problem so it can be solved.*" (W-pI.79) If we don't know what the problem is, how would we ever know to solve it?

At work, the idea here is that our *real* problem isn't the myriad of challenges we currently find on the job. Our *real* problem—and in fact the *Course* would say our *only* problem—is that we haven't cultivated the spiritual intelligence needed to see the Love in ourselves and everyone else around us. As a result, *because* we don't know who we are or who they are, the *effect* is that we don't know how to tap into our SQ in moments when we really need it—like, say, when a relationship with a colleague is threatening to rupture. Consequently, this creates a ripple effect of drama in our work lives, and we view the drama itself as the problem, *not* our own thinking that caused it.

In the next chapter, we'll explore the *Course*'s view on what's behind our most troublesome thinking, as well as how to turn the volume down on it for good. In the meantime, however, here is an exercise that will help you find the Grace the *Course* says is our true home . . . right here and now.

COURSE WORK You're not who you think you are

A while back I attended a Unity church where the guest speaker, a woman who had been a student of the *Course* for more than two decades, walked us through the following meditation. I'm sharing it here because I found it particularly valuable in transcending from the physical self we experience in our bodies to the spiritual Self we've been discussing in this chapter.

To get started, please sit in a comfortable position, either cross-legged on the floor or in a chair, with your spine tall. If it's convenient, I recommend that you dim the lights, play your favorite instrumental music, and sit quietly for a few minutes, as a way to prepare the mind for a more reflective and indwelling state.

While keeping your eyes closed, take your pointer finger and thumb from one hand and use them to pinch any finger on your other hand with enough pressure to feel a strong sting. You should squeeze to the point where your fingernails leave indents that look like tiny crescent moons, but not to the point where you break the skin (obviously).

As you let go, notice how the pain you feel is in your finger, while your experience of pain is being filtered through your mind. Now think about which one is "you" in this scenario. Are "you" the finger, the pain, or the thoughts?

The benefit of this experiment is that it demonstrates the fact that "you" aren't any of them. You're not your finger because you could lose all ten and still be alive. You're not your pain because pain is just a sensation caused by nerves and receptors of the body. And, finally, you're not your thoughts because those are just bubbles of the mind; one moment you're thinking about the pain in your finger and then—pop—that thought is gone forever.

So who are you then? From a *Course* perspective you are the perfect state of Grace beyond the thinking mind. In other words, "you" are consciousness itself, and your body is something that is happening *within you* versus "you" happening within your body.

Now, the reason any of this matters at work is because when you understand that what "you" are is so much bigger, greater, and more expansive *than* your job, it tends to bring a deep sense of peace and purpose that you can carry *to* your job. This is the SQ perspective because when you know what is eternal and true about yourself and everyone else—*interbeing*—you're not as easily yanked around by what is fleeting and false (like, for instance, the emotions that surge in you when a project goes haywire).

Along that line, the space you are accessing when you do this experiment *is* the proverbial "space between stimulus and response" where our power of decision lives. After all, what is it you're supposed to be choosing in those moments where there is a decision to be made? *The Higher Self.*

Therefore, the space you tapped into when you recognized that "you" are not your body, "you" are not your pain, and "you" are not your thoughts is the space of wisdom and compassion. This is the whole point of meditation: pulling down the Grace the *Course* says is our "natural inheritance" to the level of our direct experience. When you do this well and consistently, you cannot help but be viewed by your colleagues as growing in both maturity and leadership.

You, however, will experience this growth by its true name: Love.

KEY QUOTES

- The Self that God created needs nothing. It is forever complete, safe, loved, and loving. (From the *Course* preface, What it Says)
- You can wait, delay, paralyze yourself, or reduce your creativity to almost nothing. But you cannot abolish it. (T-1.V.1:5–6)
- Your Self does not need salvation, but your mind needs to learn what salvation is. (T-11.IV.1:3)
- The universe of love does not stop because you do not see it, nor have your closed eyes lost the ability to see. (T-11.I.5:10)

What is the ego?
Nothingness, but in
a form that seems
like something.

(C-2.2:1–2)

THE DETOUR INTO FEAR

Here's what we've learned so far in our off-roading adventure into spirituality at work: beyond the reality we all experience within our bodies, the *Course* says there is a Reality (capital "R") that is both an eternal state of Grace and perfect Love. While the *Course* doesn't attempt to analyze or further define this Reality, it does say that we can *access* it in any moment we choose.

If you participated in the Course Work exercise at the end of the last chapter, hopefully you were able to sense that there is a calm at the center of life's storms you can call upon whenever you wish. Previously, we defined this as making space to choose wisdom and compassion, which is another way of saying making space for your Higher, more spiritually intelligent, Self. In business speak, the result you're looking for here is *presence* (meaning executive presence or leadership presence), although it's important to note that presence is the *outgrowth* of spiritual intelligence and not the other way around.

This is why so many professional development programs fail to achieve the cultural change they promise. In short, they focus on external strategies and behaviors without addressing the all-important internal beliefs that drive them. No doubt this is because it's far easier to teach someone what to do than it is to teach them how to think, and yet that is precisely our goal here: to learn to think with wisdom and compassion. Or to use the *Course*'s language, to learn to think with Love.

You are not your body

Broadly speaking, if presence is making space in your mind to choose wisdom and compassion, then a *lack* of presence is created when this space feels inaccessible. Accordingly, when you can't think with Love, you can't tap into your Higher Self and, as a result, you can't behave with spiritual intelligence—or any other form of intelligence for that matter.

In my job, I've coached hundreds of professionals from many different backgrounds, and it's worth noting that there's one thing that seems to routinely block our leadership presence at work. Any guesses as to what it is? The answer is: perceived disrespect. As you've most likely experienced, there's nothing like feeling we've been ignored, slighted, or outright confronted to open the floodgates of judgment and cause a complete breakdown in composure.

This is another important distinction to make between emotional and spiritual intelligence, by the way, because if you isolate the feeling of disrespect and look at it strictly from the angle of EQ, then you will be guided to tools that regulate emotional stability. These could include a combination of deep-breathing exercises, mindfulness of body sensations, leaning into the discomfort, and so on. All of these practices are important when it comes to creating the mental white space needed for wise decision-making; still, they don't go far enough for our purposes because they don't penetrate the realm of belief.[1]

Before we go further into this idea, however, I want to pause and note that contrasting emotional and spiritual intelligence is not an attempt to undervalue the relevance of EQ. The difference I want to point out is only that while EQ is deeply entrenched in the body—and the mechanics of the brain in particular—SQ isn't related to the body at all.

This is not to say that you shouldn't learn more about your body and the neuroscience behind human behavior. In fact, when it comes to things that cause us to act unprofessionally (like perceived disrespect), it's extremely helpful to know, for example, that a body under stress sends less oxygen to the problem-solving part of the brain. This is a game-changing biological explanation for why we tend to react first and think later, and we have neuroscience to thank for it.

So, yes, as important as it is to understand the body while you're in it, it's also important from an SQ and *Course* perspective to know that you're much more than just a body. As we covered in the last chapter, this means seeing yourself as a physical being *while also* seeing yourself as part of an eternal state of Love that is connected to all life.

In chapter 1 we started developing our SQ superpowers by asking the millennia-old question, "What is God?" Having learned that the *Course*—like many other spiritual traditions—describes God as unconditional Love, let's turn our attention to why we don't feel this presence of Love in our lives each day, especially at work.

What blocks our access to Love?

To answer this question, let's define the self (lowercase "s") as the thoughts and behaviors associated with separation and self*ish*ness, which would essentially include anything that looks out for you and you alone. As a general rule, when you're thinking in terms of "I" or "my," you're referring to the lower self since this is what identifies with your job, your name, your body, and so on.

Needless to say, this does not mean that selfishness is entirely bad. After all, a certain amount of selfish thinking is beneficial because it's what motivates you to remember your home address, for example, and steer clear of dark alleys at night. That said, when selfishness is allowed to grow like a loose weed in the mind, the result is that you get tangled up in judgment and defensiveness based on whether every situation you encounter works for you *only*. This cuts off your ability to see the bigger picture and makes collaborating in teams far more difficult. In other words, too much "self" creates a blind spot that will eventually damage your reputation at work.

Now let's contrast this with the Higher Self, which we'll define here as the thoughts and actions associated with connection and self *less*ness. Note that the word *selfless* literally translates to *less self*. For our purposes this doesn't mean putting your needs below the needs of others; rather, "less self" describes the *precondition* required to experience Grace, wisdom, compassion, and Love. Think of a clogged drainpipe, for instance. If you want the water (Love) to come through, you have to unclog the pipe, which in our case means getting your lower "self" out of the way.

Now, in theory, because we know that we have the ability to access our Higher Self in any moment we choose, it should be easy to live and work in perfect inner and outer peace every day, right? That would be nice, of course, except for the fact that our experiences, not to mention our advancements in neuroscience, have proved that we often behave with *less* grace precisely in those moments when we need it most.

Why?

Welcome, friends, to the ego

While it doesn't use this exact language, the *Course* says that whenever you can't access your Higher Self it's because you have "clogged up the pipe" by choosing your own fluctuating perceptions versus allowing perfect Love and connectedness to flow through you. These perceptions are what the *Course* calls your *ego*.

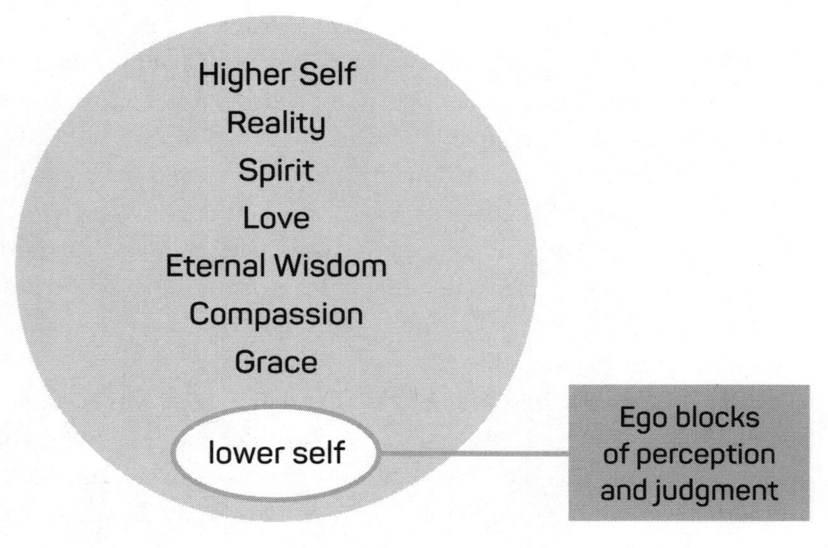

FIGURE 1

Judgments of the lower self create a barrier, blocking access to the Higher Self.

When we hear the word *ego* in work settings, it's typically associated with arrogance or an overly inflated sense of importance: *"Wow, that guy has a huge ego."* And while it's true that arrogance is certainly one *form* of the ego, it can also be said that the ego blockade to your Higher Self is capable of taking on as many forms as there are thoughts in the mind.

Let me say that again: *the ego is capable of taking on as many forms as there are thoughts in the mind.*

Frightening, isn't it? Indeed, and that's the point.

Because while the ego is just a thought, it's certainly not just any thought. The ego is a thought that the interconnected Higher Self *doesn't exist,* meaning you are all alone in a separate, deteriorating body that was created through nothing more than DNA roulette. Despite the fact that the *Course* calls this the "tiny mad idea" (T-27.VIII.6:2), the ego's job is to ensure that it feels very real to you at all times.

To put it simply, if the ego is a thought that you are separated from All that is, then this naturally produces a *cause-and-effect* relationship between ego thinking and fear. Consequently, the more disconnected from Love you feel, the more ego thoughts you have and, thus, the more fearful you become. This cycle continues to repeat itself until, eventually, the ego wall of your own judgment is so thick that your Higher Self is not only inaccessible, but often forgotten altogether.

This is why we can't access our spiritual intelligence when we need it. It's not that Grace isn't available to us; it's that we're too distracted by the incessant noise of our own churning mind, and it's the *noise* we tend to focus on, not its underlying cause. Again, think about what happens when you perceive yourself to be disrespected at work and lose all sense of presence. This occurs when you react based on the concerns of the lower self (*how does this affect me?*) versus responding with the wisdom and compassion of the Higher Self (*what is the most loving thought available in this moment?*).

We'll go further into the specifics of how to respond to the ego in upcoming chapters, but first I want to answer a couple of questions that surface quite a bit at this point when I'm consulting with professionals who are trying to incorporate *Course* principles in the workplace.

Where did the ego come from?

While the *Course* doesn't detail the precise origins of ego thinking, I can say that if you look closely enough, it doesn't take long to see how patterns of division have been playing out in our lives from the very beginning. We practically come out of the womb using the word *mine*, which means that from the moment we are able to view the world through a lens of what is "ours" and "not ours," there is a fear in us—even as children—that we won't have enough. These thoughts of separation and competition are continually reinforced as we grow into adulthood, which only strengthens the fear, which strengthens the ego, which strengthens the division until, again, it doesn't take long before ego thinking becomes all we know.

In fact, look around at the ways you are conditioned to see separation every day—in gender, race, nationality, religion, economic status, political parties, and so on—and then consider how much judgment arises from these "differences" as a result. Try to go through a full day paying close attention to how much of what you are exposed to in advertising, on social media, in the news—and definitely at work—either subtly or not so subtly encourages you to blame, judge, and compare yourself to others. Now multiply this by the number of days you've been alive and you'll no longer wonder why we've become so competitive and disconnected.

Is the ego the same as "the devil" or "evil"?

Given how destructive ego thinking can be, you may assume that it's some kind of external, sinister "devil" or a force synonymous with "evil" at work in the world. From a *Course* perspective there's no such thing as the devil—nothing Real can be threatened and nothing unreal exists, remember? However, the *Course* does acknowledge that the depth of our *belief* in the ego causes us to behave in evil ways.

The mind can make the belief in separation very real and very fearful, and this belief is the "devil."

(T-3.VII.5:1)

For our purposes, the reason this matters is because it means that "hell" isn't something saved for when we die; *it's something we're choosing to experience here and now.* In other words, with every unloving thought of separation, with every judgment, and with every missed opportunity to connect to your Higher Self, the *Course* says you bring hell right into the present where it becomes your direct experience.

As an example, think of a time in your life when your anger, judgment, or fear was so intense and so raging that you felt completely out of control. What was going through your mind in those moments? How did you feel about yourself? How did you behave as a result and what impact did your behavior have on those around you?

Is this not hell?

Now consider the fact that scientists estimate we have fifty thousand thoughts per day on average, and as many as two hundred thousand thoughts per day when we're under stress. If we define the ego as a thought of fear, then what percentage of these thoughts are we using to create or reinforce our own suffering? Along that line, I'm sure it's safe to assume that the dramatic spike in thinking we display under stress isn't the result of positive mantras. Indeed, it's most likely the result of useless ruminations on the very things that caused us to be stressed in the first place.

Just knowing that we have at least fifty thousand thoughts per day should be reason enough not to identify too closely with any one of them—and yet we do, much to our own individual and collective unhappiness. Again I'll ask, *Is this not hell?*

If you agree, then it's time for us to take responsibility for what's happening within our own minds. In other words, the devil did not make us do it. *Our own thoughts of fear did.* The ones caused by deep wounds, insecurities, guilt, shame, jealousies, judgment, and power quests that clog our thinking and block our access to Grace. Avoiding, denying, or blaming these thoughts on an evil force or a retrograde planet doesn't make them go away. In fact, not only does that *not* work but, worse, the *Course* says the very ego thoughts we try to hide or evade often become the ones that stalk us the most. As the saying goes, *"What we resist persists."*

How do you get rid of the ego?

When it comes to dismantling the ego, the first step is to understand that, since every experience begins with a thought, this means changing your experience begins with changing your mind about it. For instance, let's say you work in a job that you don't particularly enjoy, but you show up because it pays the bills, provides health insurance, and—more to the point—you don't have a better option at the moment. In this situation, an unchecked ego would take any opportunity to make each day completely miserable and thus keep you stuck in "hell."

Accordingly, what kind of experience do you think you'd have with thoughts like these?

"This place sucks."

"I hate everyone here."

"I'm wasting my time."

"I'm stuck."

Now picture your day with fifty thousand more of those same thoughts. In all likelihood, you'd arrive at work annoyed before you even walk through the door, alienate everyone around you, and feel even more alone and unhappy as a result. See the ego spiral here? Instead, by taking responsibility for your own thinking, you discover that you can be in the exact same situation while having a *completely different experience of it* depending on whether you are looking through the lens of the ego or through the lens of spiritual intelligence.

The exercise below is a terrific first step in this process because it provides a framework for *witnessing* and *naming* the most common blocks that keep us stuck in the small self. In future chapters, we will take steps to heal these blocks as we continue our journey through the *Course*.

COURSE WORK Where are your thoughts?

Sane judgment would inevitably judge against the ego, and must be obliterated by the ego in the interest of its self-preservation.

(T-4.V.1:6)

This is a very practical tool I use with my Awake Exec: Mindful Wisdom at Work coaching clients that is designed to help the group get honest about the kind of thinking that dominates their head space. The idea here is very simple: all you have to do is keep the following chart beside you for at least a full day (three to four days is ideal) and, whenever you observe yourself having a thought in one of the four quadrants listed, make a note by placing a dot in that area. (For a printable version of this tool, visit miraclesatworkbook.com.)

Keep in mind that this exercise is for your whole day, not just your time at work, because it will be revealing for you to witness whether your habitual thinking patterns change in different environments. Are you more emotional at work but more future-focused at home, or vice versa? Do you carry work home and allow it to distract you from being fully present? Do you bring your personal life to work? Collectively, what does this experiment say about your "default" mental state?

Please note that when filling in your dots, it's important to remember that you're not being asked to analyze anything while completing the exercise itself. Whether you experiment with this for one day or one week, the only thing you have to do is make a quick and truthful assessment of where your thoughts are for a specific period of time. This should take only a few seconds whenever you do it—but it's very important that you do it consistently. It's also important that you don't force yourself to think a certain way in order to manipulate the results. This exercise is for your eyes only, and the more honest you are, the more you will benefit from the process.

After you have filled in the sheet for at least a twenty-four-hour period, you should be able to (literally) connect the dots and visualize where you are stuck and where you are clinging to fear and limiting beliefs. As an example, if you are experiencing a lot of anger or disappointment, it could be because you're viewing the present through the filter of your past. Likewise, if you're experiencing a lot of overthinking or impatience, it could be because you're worried about the future and anxious about things you can't control.

Regardless of what you learn from this exercise, remember that the purpose of the *Course* is to train the mind to think with Love, and Love begins with yourself. This means if you have more dots in the past, future, or emotional quadrants—as most people do—please do not allow it to serve as an excuse for judging your professional competence or your spiritual progression. Instead, let it serve as a gentle reminder of the areas where your lower self needs to step aside, and know that you couldn't have even gotten this far if you didn't have enough courage to look. So let's get started.

Past ("*If only . . .* ")

Place a dot in this box each time you find yourself feeling any sort of anger, guilt, or related emotion about something that has already happened. This includes perpetually rehashing old events, holding "grudgements" (i.e., judging a person in the present for past behaviors), or wishing the past were different so your present could be "better."

TOTAL ___________

Future ("*What if . . .* ")

Place a dot in this box each time you find yourself feeling anxious about things that haven't happened yet. This includes worrying about the future of your finances, your career, your health, your family—anything that has your mind projecting ahead and feeling nervous about what you could find there.

TOTAL ___________

Emotional ("*What the . . . ?*")	**Strategic ("*What now . . . ?*")**
Place a dot in this box each time you find yourself spinning into an emotional reaction about something that is happening right now. This includes feelings of anger toward a particular person, frustration toward a specific situation, or just general unrest about your circumstances in this moment.	***Place a dot in this box each time you find yourself "sticking with the facts."*** This means separating the data from any emotions or judgments, and looking for solutions to the day's events with calm and logic.
TOTAL ___________	TOTAL ___________

Over what period of time did you do this exercise (one day, two days, five days, etc.)?

In which quadrant did you find yourself placing the most dots?

What do your current patterns of thought tell you about where your potential blocks are related to accessing the Grace available to you?

KEY QUOTES

- Your denial made no change in what you are. But you have split your mind into what knows and does not know the truth. (W-pI.139.5:3–4)

- Your mind can be possessed by illusions, but spirit is eternally free. (T-1.IV.2:8)

- Thoughts are not big or little, powerful or weak. They are merely true or false. Those that are true create their own likeness. Those that are false make theirs. (W-pI.16.1:4–7)

- You would not excuse insane behavior on your part by saying you could not help it. Why should you condone insane thinking? (T-2.VI.2:2–3)

- The ego arose from the separation, and its continued existence depends on your continuing belief in the separation. (T-4.III.3:2)

We look inside first,
decide the kind of
world we want to see
and then project that
world outside, making
it the truth *as we see it.*

COURSE **PREFACE, WHAT IT SAYS**

SPIRITUAL INTELLIGENCE BLOCK #1

Projection Makes Perception

Now that you know more about what the ego *is*—namely, a thought of fear that arises when you feel disconnected from Love—let's look a bit closer at what the ego *does*. In the next three chapters we're going to cover three of the primary ways egoic thinking serves as a block to your Higher Self/spiritual intelligence and, thus, blocks your access to wisdom and compassion at work. As you continue to take the broad metaphysical framework of the *Course* and apply it to your career, it's important that you not only know what these ego patterns are, but that you can recognize when they're coming up in your own mind. Again, even though the ego is nothing more than a thought, it's a thought with the ability to drive supremely unwise behavior if you allow it.

Penny for your thoughts

To begin, take a look at your sheet from the Where Are Your Thoughts? exercise in the last chapter. Imagine that you have to hold a penny for every egoic past, future, or emotional thought listed. For example, if you have thirty dots that reflect some form of ego thinking, then this would mean that you have thirty pennies to hold.

Now let's assume you have another round of ego thinking tomorrow, and so you are given another thirty pennies. The next day you pick up thirty more, and another thirty after that, until what began as a fairly easy task has become totally unbearable. Eventually, you reach a point where the burden of the extra weight becomes all-consuming and you can no longer think about anything else.

So what do you do? Naturally, you're going to try to get rid of your pennies, which, as it turns out, is precisely what we need to do with the "real" pennies of our ego. In other words, sooner or later that fear-based thinking simply becomes too heavy to keep to ourselves.

Enter projection

In the *Course*, the ego's chief tool for keeping fear out of your mind is *projection*, which essentially means shifting the responsibility for your own thoughts and actions to something external and, hence, away from your direct control. The idea here is that if you are at the effect of other people or circumstances, you are spared from looking at your own thinking as the cause of anything that happens in your life.

Becoming aware of your projections is a major theme in the *Course*, to the point where it even says that everything you see is "the outside picture of an inward condition." (T-21.In.1:5) As an example, you might think you're experiencing a sense of anger because of something that is happening *to* you, but the *Course* says you're actually angry because it's coming *from* you. It's *your own* angry thoughts that you're trying to avoid by projecting them onto something "outside." But since there is no "outside" in the spiritual sense, all you're really doing is circulating the energy of anger versus dissolving it entirely.

This is why the *Course* says you can't solve a problem until you recognize what really *is* the problem. Until you understand that the real issue is the fear within your own mind, you will continue to look out into the world for solutions and wonder why nothing ever changes.

How to recognize projection thoughts

Now that you know what projection is, the next step is to know when you're doing it. Obviously, because projection is a product of thought, it can take an unlimited number of forms. That said, the good news is all projection essentially boils down to one of these two mental potholes:

"I'm (feeling) because (insert event)."
or
"I (decided this) because (insert behavior of another person)."

To give you some examples of projection in action, here's a small sampling from my coaching clients over the years:

I sent that heated email *because* she cut my budget.

I was rude in that meeting *because* he was rude to me first.

I raid the fridge at night *because* I'm awake answering emails.

Do you see how the second half of the sentence doesn't necessarily connect to the first? For instance, the client raiding the refrigerator presumes her behavior *is the result* of being up late but that's just not true. If it were, then everyone who happened to be up at the same time would have the same compulsion. Likewise, it's not true that everyone who has their budget cut will automatically send a nasty email, and so on.

The conclusion here is that the *feelings and behavior* in the first half of the sentence are tied to *the meaning projected* onto the second half. This is where the tools you've learned so far can be highly valuable. As you begin to understand the often deceptive relationship you have with your own thoughts, you become much better at separating the facts of a situation from the emotions attached to it. Stripping off the emotion is what deepens your ability to be present in the moment, and that is what opens space in your mind for wiser, more compassionate decisions.

The happy trap

When it comes to projection, it's important to note that according to the *Course* it is just as easy—and just as dangerous—to project your *happiness* as it is to project your anger or sadness. This means if your ability to be happy depends on another person or an external condition, then even if everything is going well for now, it's still a form of the ego because you will always have the fear that what "completes" you could be taken away at any moment.

Remember: the presence of fear *is* the ego and, specifically, the thoughts of separation. Accordingly, you can (and should) be off-the-charts happy for the beautiful gifts in your life—a great kid, a great job, a great partner—but you're strapping in for an emotional roller coaster if you make any one of those things the source of your joy. This is because every heart-bursting moment of bliss you feel will be accompanied by an equally heart-breaking moment of panic, whether you're consciously aware of it or not. This panic is the result of the *fear* that comes with knowing at the deepest level that what you depend on for your happiness will one day be separated from you.

At work, this kind of projection often manifests as competition and insecurity. For example, you may celebrate when you land the deal, but somewhere in the back of your mind you know there's always someone up-and-coming behind you who will take your spotlight tomorrow. As a result, you keep chasing your own life—always running toward the next goal and always focused on how you look from the "outside." If this sounds familiar, it's the fear you're running from, whether this fear lives in you as a dull hum just below the surface or flares up in monstrous rage. Either way, when you feel it, you'll do anything you can to get rid of it.

Creating what you defend against

Clearly, if projection is shifting responsibility for your pain or your happiness onto something external, then you must naturally maintain a certain amount of defensiveness in order to feel "safe." After all, you have to be defensive *against* what you believe can harm you and be defensive *of* what you cherish. Over time, this need to be protective on both fronts becomes like a heavy suit of armor (or a heavy bag of pennies), and, ironically, the *Course* says, it's your defensiveness that creates an even greater need to defend yourself.

Think about the last time you had a conversation with a colleague that went completely into the ditch. Chances are, at some point one of you got defensive, which caused the other person to get more aggressive, and the next thing you knew there was tension. At an intellectual level, we all understand that these situations aren't helpful, but they tend to escalate much faster than we have time to process them.

Still, a quick way to catch yourself in projection—particularly during heated discussions—is when you can feel that your goal in the situation is to *win* versus finding the space for compassion and wisdom. After all, if you're coming from the ego place of separation, then you're coming from a belief that in order for you to "win," the other person has to lose. This means that even if you do get what you want in the end, it's not a victory to be savored for long because your attack will only create more resentment and retaliation on all sides. As the *Course* says, you are actually *creating* the very thing that you're attempting to defend yourself against. *Is this strength?* In the world perhaps, but remember: we're invoking a Love beyond this world.

COURSE WORK Unwinding projection

You respond to what you perceive,
and as you perceive so shall you behave.

(T-1.III.6:1)

Years ago I was listening to a speaker being challenged by an audience member who was complaining about the myriad of ways she felt stuck in her career. What caught my attention was that every time the speaker suggested a possible action step or path forward, the woman immediately found some way to shoot it down.

"I've already tried that."
"That would never work."

"My boss wouldn't let me."
"My husband doesn't support me."

Finally the speaker said, "*It's not that you don't know what to do—it's that you're not ready to fully own what you know.*"

It was a brilliant response and one that goes right to the core of why we choose the egoic thoughts of projection and, thus, choose our own hell. Sometimes it's not that we don't know what to do; it's that acting on what we know would force us to change in ways that are uncomfortable. As a result, our brain—which has evolved to keep us alive, not to actualize our potential—then interprets our discomfort as a threat. Next, in order to keep us "safe," our mind begins searching for excuses as to why stretching into the unknown is a terrible idea. This happens at lightning speed, by the way, which means that oftentimes what feels like sound judgment in the moment is actually just the ego's fear in disguise. In other words, it's another form of the little self cutting off access to the Higher Self.

Projection comes in when we know that staying in our current situation is living much smaller than we feel called to live. Thus, in order to justify our unwillingness to change, we find another person or circumstance to blame for it. This doesn't work, of course, because, again, we only wind up creating the very thing we're attempting to defend against. In the case of the woman above who felt blocked in her career, for example, her defensiveness around being stuck *was the very thing keeping her stuck.*

Accordingly, your challenge for today is to notice the ways in which projection arises in your own mind and, specifically, what triggered this reaction. Where are you attempting to ease your own discomfort by placing the blame on someone else at work? Where are you not taking full responsibility for what you're feeling? Where are you stymied by overthinking in a way that prevents you from taking action? Please take a few moments to write what comes to you in the space provided.

KEY QUOTES

- Deceive yourself no longer that you are helpless in the face of what is done to you. (T-21.II.2:6)
- Suffering is an emphasis upon all that the world has done to injure you. (T-27.VII.1:1)
- The ego believes that power, understanding and truth lie in separation, and to establish this belief it must attack. (T-11.V.13:4)
- Mistake not the intensity of rage projected fear must spawn. (W-pI.161.8:3)
- Your Self is still in peace, even though your mind is in conflict. You have not yet gone back far enough, and that is why you become so fearful. (T-3.VII.5:8–9)

Pursuit of specialness
is always at the cost
of peace.

(T-24.II.2:1)

SPIRITUAL INTELLIGENCE BLOCK #2

Specialness: The Great Dictator of the Wrong Decisions

Because the ideology of *A Course in Miracles* is new to so many—and applying its lessons to your career is even more unfamiliar—let's quickly recap the highlights of our journey to this point.

1. **The reality of oneness**
   Only the part of us that cannot die is real. This is our spiritual Source—defined in the Course *as Love—which is shared by all living things.*

2. **The perception of separation**
   Falling asleep to spiritual Source, we look to our separate bodies and to the world for love and completion.

3. **Fear and projection**
   Making external conditions responsible for our internal wholeness generates an enormous amount of fear, which we attempt to remove from our *mind by projecting it onto others. This fear—which the* Course *calls ego—only reinforces our experience of suffering.*

As you can see, things really begin to go downhill for us the moment we perceive that our oneness has been broken. Not only does this introduce the idea of *relationship* to our perspective (after all, now we can judge and compare ourselves against other "selves") but it also introduces the concept of *lack*: Who has more? Who has less? Who's going to get the big promotion? Who's going to get passed over? Who has the boss's ear? Who is out of the loop?

From a *Course* perspective, we lose regardless of whether we think we have more or less because the ego will always meet us exactly where we are. In other words, if we believe that we are "less than" someone else, the ego will show up as scarcity mentality or a sense of being incomplete. Likewise, if we believe that we are "better than," the ego will morph into a sense that we could lose what we treasure at any minute, sending us falling back into the arms of fear.

Either way, the message we've bought into here is that we're not whole already. So, to make up for our internal feelings of lack, oftentimes we attempt to use external prizes to fill the void. In the workplace these external prizes include job titles, salaries and raises, managing the plum clients, getting the best office, making the best deals—and on and on it goes.

Something special

In the *Course*, anything we place between (or use as a substitute for) the peace, wisdom, and compassion that come from Love is defined as a *special relationship* or *specialness*. Like projection, specialness keeps our focus on what is *outside* in an effort to avoid the inner work required for true spiritual intelligence. Also like projection, specialness can include things that make us happy (this is called "special love") as well as things that trigger us into defensiveness and judgment (this is "special hate"). In some cases, you can even have both special love and special hate toward the same thing, such as a professional or personal relationship gone sour, for instance. At first the person was your "savior," but then they became your target.

Specialness can be particularly dangerous when it comes to your career because, if you attach your sense of identity and completion to what happens at work, then by definition you are hooking into a "source" that is constantly changing. *Did you meet the sales numbers or not? Did you get the promotion or not? Does the boss like you or not?* These thoughts will strap you back into the emotional roller coaster of being content in one moment and anxious the next, affecting how you interact with others and, thus, the quality of your relationships and reputation on the job and beyond.

Learning about specialness the hard way

A few years ago I found myself in a *deeply* special relationship with my own career in the sense that I had far too much self-worth wrapped up in what I was (and wasn't) achieving. When things were working out, like a major media hit or a big speaking engagement, I was over-the-moon thrilled. However, when things didn't work out, I allowed my disappointment to bleed into other areas of my life. In particular, I became very impatient with my children.

The turning point came one morning when I was trying to hurry my two boys out the door for school. We were running late that day and I remember yelling at my five-year-old to put on his shoes.

Then, I yelled at my six-year-old to find his backpack.

Then, I yelled at *both* of them to get in the car.

And as I slammed the door, jerked the gearshift into reverse, and turned around to pull out of the driveway, I noticed my oldest son crying in the backseat. His face was red, and he clenched his body tightly as he stared at the floor, tears streaming down his cheeks.

"*Mommy*," he said, "*You make me sad*."

That was it. No screaming. No tantrum. Just a child who was clearly hurting.

Oy vey.

The tantrums I can handle but this—*this*—was something else entirely. I looked over at his brother, who met my eyes briefly, and then also stared coldly at the ground.

Without a word, I put the car in park, grabbed the steering wheel with both hands, and sat there in shocked silence. In that moment a wave of guilt and shame crashed over me and . . . I lost it. I buried my face in my hands and had a good old-fashioned, red-eyed, runny-nose, ugly cry.

Eventually I took a couple of deep breaths, turned completely around in the seat, and reached out to both of them.

"Take my hands," I said.

They each grabbed the tips of my fingers.

"I'm sorry. I shouldn't have yelled at you. I don't know what's wrong with me, but I promise I'm going to figure it out and get better, okay?"

They nodded, but it was still an awkwardly silent ride to school.

It is never the idol that you want

I learned in that moment why the *Course* calls specialness "the great dictator of the wrong decisions." (T-24.I.5:1) Because if we *start* from a place where feeling complete is wrapped up in something outside—career accomplishments, another person, numbers in the bank—our behaviors will run the gamut from self-pity to manipulation to attack in order to get and keep what we want. Our decisions then become motivated *not* by wisdom or compassion, but by desperation and control, which typically causes us to lose the very things we've made our idol, sending us back into the world to numb the pain.

Sound familiar?

Sadly, for so many of us, this pattern not only robs our peace, but it's also the root cause of crippling addictions—from relationship, food, work, and technology addictions all the way to drug and alcohol dependency. And through it all, as we "strain to hear [the] soundless voice" (T-24.II.4:6) of the world, the memory of who we really are drifts farther . . . and farther . . . and farther from our awareness.

Everything you have taught yourself has made your power more and more obscure to you. You know not what it is, nor where.

(T-14.XI.1:5–6)

Compounding this problem is the fact that, as we frantically chase after the idols we've made special, we become blind to the fact that *pursuit itself is another trap*. This is when we fall into what the *Course* calls "elusive happiness" (T-21.VII.13:1), meaning we start to believe that we're just *one goal away* from the attainment of true bliss and fulfillment. This in turn creates a never-ending spiral of *when-thens*, where success is always within eyesight yet always just out of reach. When it comes to your career, it might go like this:

When I get a new job, **then** I'll be happy.

When I get promoted, **then** I'll be happy.

When I become the boss, **then** I'll be happy.

When I earn more money, **then** I'll be happy.

When my peers respect me, **then** I'll be happy.

When I become famous, **then** I'll be happy.

These thoughts obviously extend to areas outside of work as well, such as:

When the disease is gone, **then** I'll be happy.

When I meet the right partner, **then** I'll be happy.

When I have a baby, **then** I'll be happy.

When I lose the weight, **then** I'll be happy, and so on.

And yet, as the *Course* reminds us, "It is never the idol that you want, but what you think it offers you." (T-30.III.4:1–2) In other words, we've become so busy hunting down our desired *form* of success that we fail to see what we're *really* after is the sense of completion we expect that success to provide. It's the *completion*—which is just another word for Love—that we're seeking, and we're mindlessly searching for it in a world where it cannot be found.

"Seek but do not find" remains the world's stern decree, and no one who pursues the world's goals can do otherwise.

(M-13.5:8)

If our success is measured by a source that is constantly in flux, then how can we not always be grasping? Moreover, what happens when the job is gone, the fame eludes us, the baby doesn't arrive, or the cancer spreads? The *Course* says that if we make any external source of happiness our "idol," when those idols fall we will fall with them—and we will fall hard.

Therefore, the cure for specialness according to the *Course* is to know—first and foremost—that you have access to an eternal, changeless core of Love that remains perfect regardless of what shifts and changes around you. In fact, the *Course*'s response to our pursuit of "shadows attached to nothing" (T-21.VII.12:6) is to gently remind us that whenever we do allow ourselves to feel lack in any way, we are choosing to believe that this Love is imperfect and therefore so are we.

As always, our *behaviors* can be imperfect (and often are) but the important thing to remember here is that behaviors occur *at the level of the body*, not the spirit. It's at *this* level, the spiritual level of belief, that the *Course* is asking you to make a choice: you can choose to believe that you were created perfectly whole *or* you can believe that you are imperfect and thus have every reason to feel deprived, competitive, alone, and afraid. These are the two thought systems available to you, and when you become fearful, it's clear which one you have chosen.

Whenever there is fear, it is because you have not made up your mind. Your mind is therefore split, and your behavior inevitably becomes erratic.

(T-2.VI.5:8–9)

Your Self is still at peace

From a career perspective this means that whatever you achieve (or don't achieve) pales in comparison to how you hold it. In other words, *everything* about how you carry yourself and present yourself at work is its own teaching on who you believe you are as well as who you believe everyone else is. If you believe that your identity is defined by what you do, then that's your choice to make. But expect that choice to come with a tremendous amount of anxiety as you measure your worth against whether you hit the "right" goal or make the "right" people like you. Moreover, expect that choice to come with a fair amount of interpersonal friction as you compete with and judge others based on where they fall in meeting your needs. Again, these are all your decisions to make, but you pay for them with your own sense of peace.

On the other hand, the more you turn away from the up-and-down insanity of specialness and turn toward your changeless core of Love, the more sanity you will bring to your work and to those around you. We'll go deeper into the specifics of how to do that in the next section, but for now just think about how differently you would carry yourself in the office if you knew—as in, *really knew*—your true Self as Love and were capable of seeing others as extensions of this same Source. Think about what a difference in aura and energy you would carry to your job and how unmoved and unthreatened you would be by any chaos that surrounds you or circumstances you can't control. Now imagine the effect your presence would have on colleagues who see you as a model of composure, and the impact that would have on your influence and the dynamic of your culture and your teams.

All of this is possible and, as it says in the *Course*, waiting only for you to choose it.

And yet, the fact that we take great pains to continue our search for internal completion in external things implies that maybe it's not such a simple choice after all. As you'll learn in the next chapter, maybe we've been given everything, *but what happens if we don't really want it*?

COURSE WORK Preference vs. investment

A thousand homes he makes,
yet none contents his restless mind.
(W-PI.182.3:3)

Course teacher Kenneth Wapnick often spoke about the difference between investment and preference, noting that we should be aware of our *preferences* for certain people, cities, food, clothes, art, spiritual practices, and so forth without having an *investment* in them. Since investment is the breeding ground for specialness, your task for today is to consider the many ways our identities are built around what the world claims is important—and how this practice drives us deeper and deeper into fragmented, ego-based thinking.

For example, consider how we pay extra for "special" treatment, how we celebrate "special" occasions, how companies give "special" perks, how inquiring relatives ask if you've met anyone "special" yet, and the list goes on. Next, consider how you've been invested in *your own* specialness as a means of self-worth and get curious about what arises for you.

When it comes to your career, it will also be helpful to think about how you've made *other* people "special"—either through your adoration (special love) or your contempt (special hate)—and how this has made you feel as a result. What happens within your own mind when you put a colleague, employee, or boss above or beneath you, and how does this affect your behavior when you're around them? Getting curious about ways in which you tilt relationships—and in which direction you tilt them—can lead to some very powerful discoveries about your own sense of self-worth and where your "investments" are placed.

Accordingly, please take five minutes and freewrite what comes to you in the space below. Don't stop or edit yourself during the process; just set a timer and commit to keeping your pen on the page from start to finish. This is one of the most beneficial exercises for outing the ego and bringing thoughts of separation to the forefront of your awareness, so don't skip it. The insights you gain will be well worth five minutes of your time.

KEY QUOTES

- Every special relationship you have made has, as its fundamental purpose, the aim of occupying your mind so completely that you will not hear the call of truth. (T-17.IV.3:3)
- Do not deceive yourself into believing that you can relate in peace to God or to your brothers with anything external. (T-1.VII.1:7)
- We have observed before how many senseless things have seemed to you to be salvation. (W-pI.76.1:1)
- The prayer for things of this world will bring experiences of this world. (M-21.3:1)
- . . . all special relationships have elements of fear in them. This is why they shift and change so frequently. They are not based on changeless love alone. And love, where fear has entered, cannot be depended on because it is not perfect. (T-15.V.4:1–4)

Truth cannot deal with errors that you want.

(T-3.IV.7:2)

SPIRITUAL INTELLIGENCE BLOCK #3

The Need to Self-Sabotage

Jo is the president and CEO of a regional bank that was hit hard during the recession. After years of record-breaking profits, a string of slow returns forced her into mass layoffs—including that of her own stepfather—and the fallout not only demoralized the remaining staff, but it also earned her the nickname "hatchet lady" around the office.

Publicly, Jo tried to put on a brave face (if only to convince the creditors), but behind closed doors she seriously doubted her ability to cope with the stress and demands of her position.

As if that wasn't bad enough, the board of directors began to turn on her.

"There was one person in particular who really wanted me fired," she told me. "He would say the most horrible things in front of everyone, things that are still too painful to repeat."

After a meeting during which this board member (I'll call him Larry) was especially brutal, Jo asked me what she should do.

"Pray for his happiness," I told her.

The look of pure nausea on Jo's face said it all.

"You've *got* to be kidding me," she replied. "I could never do that."

Getting to one(ness)

Let's consider what's between the peace Jo could experience, even in the middle of a supremely difficult time, and what she was actually feeling—which in this case was thinly veiled wrath, driven by a wellspring of hurt and fear. When I asked Jo to define what was making her so angry, her immediate response was to point out Larry's *behavior*, specifically the way he yelled during their meetings and disparaged her in public.

"There's no way to sugarcoat this," she told me. "It's a war."

I understood what Jo was saying, and I also understood why she assumed this was no time for spiritual intelligence. My job, however, was to convince her otherwise.

To begin, I wanted to get Jo to a place where she was willing to see the spiritual perfection in Larry. I asked her to repeat a series of questions to herself, privately and meditatively throughout the day, and to continue this exercise until she could honestly answer yes to each of them. The questions were:

1. *Can you see the changeless core that* ***exists*** *in him?*

2. *Can you see that the changeless core in him is* ***perfect*** *despite his outward behavior?*

3. *Can you see that the changeless core in him is* ***shared*** *with you?*

After about a week of practicing, taking one step forward and two steps backward at times, Jo begrudgingly got to a place where she could acknowledge the spiritual connectedness she shared with Larry. At first this was all she was willing to do, but it was enough to create a tiny patch of spiritual ground, and so for a while we simply planted ourselves there.

Slowly (very slowly), a break of daylight emerged in her thinking when she recognized that underneath Larry's actions was a man, an all-too-human being, who was fearful about his situation too. In fact, she understood for the first time that it was *only* an extreme amount of fear that would cause someone to behave the way he did.

While processing this breakthrough, Jo told me that she was "choosing to see through his behavior to the Truth of who he is, and to see his actions as a call for love."

Jo had not yet reached the point of being able to pray for Larry's happiness, but she *was* able to be around him without shrinking or puffing up, a new development we both considered remarkable progress. That said, even though she had touched the power and presence that spiritual intelligence provides, she still couldn't manage to hold it consistently. There were moments when Larry got under her skin, and when that happened, she wasn't shy about letting him know.

The first obstacle to peace

I mentioned before that whenever I asked Jo to define what made her angry, she immediately pointed to Larry's behavior. I let this slide while Jo was genuinely trying to see him as one with her, but now that she had made some headway in that area, it was time to address it in earnest.

In the *Course*, there's a wonderful section of the text called The Obstacles to Peace (T-19.IV), where the first obstacle is defined as "our desire to get rid of it." Like Jo, you might be confused by this language and wonder why anyone would want to "get rid" of peace. Yet our behaviors tell a different story, don't they? In Jo's case, she was *choosing* to abandon her peace every time she projected her anger and fear onto Larry, making him responsible for how she felt and the behaviors she displayed as a result.

Jo understood this at an intellectual level; the problem was she didn't understand how to change.

The illusion of thought

Maybe you haven't had to fight for your job as fiercely or as publicly as Jo did, but I'm guessing you've had moments where fear-based behaviors have resulted in conflict or, at the very least, blocked your ability to be composed under pressure. In other words, moments when you have "gotten rid of" your peace.

And yet, if the judgments and fear that keep you in "hell" are nothing more than thoughts, *you should be able to dismiss them whenever you choose*. After all, thoughts aren't manifest until you act on them, which means that (in theory at least) it should be just as easy to shift your thinking about something as "big" as, say, a board member trying to get you fired as it would be to shift your thinking about something as "small" as where to eat lunch.

If you're scratching your head, perhaps it will help to look at it this way: If I asked you to touch your nose right now, you could. Likewise, if I asked you to touch your belly button right now, presumably you could do that too. However, if I asked you to touch your *fear* right now, you couldn't. That's because fear doesn't "exist." It *feels* real when you're swimming in it, but upon closer inspection, there's nothing to swim in but your own thoughts. These thoughts aren't even real unless you engage with them, so the fact that you willingly cling to thoughts that don't serve you must mean that on some level *you want to keep them*. The elephant-in-the-room question here is why: *Why would you consistently choose to make your own hell if you knew that getting out of it would be as simple as changing your mind?* In Jo's case, why *wouldn't* she want to pray for Larry's happiness if she knew that at the deepest level his happiness was tied to her own?

The most special relationship (is with your "self")

It's clear that our aversion and "unwillingness to learn" (T-31.I.1:6) a perspective of oneness and interbeing stems from the fact that we *like* our individual identities. In other words, we like to see *our* bodies, *our* families, and *our* friends as special. We like to see *our* name on the certificate and *our* title on the door. And, if we're really being honest, we have to admit that we also like measuring ourselves against others because we're biologically programmed to win. At the end of the day, "winners" are the ones who have better jobs, better houses, and better vacations—not to mention a vastly improved dating pool, thereby increasing the odds of passing on genes to future generations of winners.

Accordingly, if we don't agree to the terms of the *Course*'s plan for our happiness—acknowledging the interconnectedness of all things—then why would we ever drop the judgments that would make achieving that plan possible? No, thanks—we'll keep the hell.

Of course, this is where the problem arises because, in order to keep our judgments and our separate self, *we must get rid of the peace*. In other words, we have to sabotage ourselves daily by making what the *Course* calls a "decision to forget" (T-10.II) our true Self (capital "S") and keep the perception of separation going. As such, we don't just have an *urge* to judge: we have a *need* to do it.

The second obstacle to peace

This brings us to the second obstacle to peace, which the *Course* defines as "the attraction of guilt." (T-19.IV) Simply put, we're attracted to the idea of *other people* bearing the guilt for a bad situation because it takes the blame off us. This gives us the best of both worlds: we get to keep our specialness and projections without ever recognizing them as the cause of our pain. Returning to our previous example, if Larry is at fault because he's always stirring things up with his belligerent behavior, this takes Jo off the hook in her mind. After all, *she* isn't the one creating the hell she's stuck in, *he* is.

Yet if you wish to be the author of reality,
you will insist on holding on to judgment.

(T-3.VI.5:8)

To recap, if judging something means perceiving it as separate, and if separation means you get the power to "author your own reality," then *you've got a vested interest in judging everything you see, all the time*. When you judge something as good, you get to feel in control. ("I" made this happen.) When you judge something as bad, you get to be the victim. (It's "their" fault.) Either way, you get to keep your "self"—small "s"—which has been the goal all along.

How to self-*meditate*

Despite being confronted by the obstacles to peace, Jo was making progress in acknowledging her spiritual interconnectedness with Larry.

The changeless core questions mentioned earlier were beginning to have an effect; however, she still found herself undergoing intense bouts of judgment and anger that she couldn't seem to shake. This was when we decided to go deeper into self-*meditation*, meaning a daily practice of five-minute reflections that I "prescribed" for her. Instead of attempting to ignore her frustrations or bitterly vent to anyone who'd listen, Jo began by visualizing herself and Larry surrounded by rays of white light, symbolizing their shared spirit. Next, she prayed for healing thoughts and, finally, even though she had to work up to it, she prayed for Larry's happiness.

Jo repeated this practice every day until, eventually, her anger lifted to the point where she was able to pleasantly acknowledge the success of one of Larry's projects in a board meeting, much to the amazement of everyone else in the room.

No seething. No dirty looks. No thinly veiled sarcasm. Just a spiritual intelligence that had grown strong enough to recognize that her anger was making a bad situation far worse, and that regardless of his behavior, Larry was host to the same presence of Love that was found in her.

Jo's relationship with Larry improved dramatically, and even now, eight years later, she is still CEO and he's still on the board of directors. They don't socialize after work—or even much during work for that matter—but the underlying animosity is gone, and the bank is once again highly profitable.

"Best of all, I'm no longer the hatchet lady," she joked to me one day.

It's easy to look at Jo's story and think she "won" because she got to keep her job, and while that's true, there's a much bigger and more important win here that can be summarized in Gandhi's famous quote, "As the means so the end." Jo recognized that if the *path* she chose through the bank's recovery was one of anger and resentment, then her *destination* would be those things too. I would even argue that if her path had been to continually get rid of her peace by seeing the guilt in others, her destination would have been very different indeed.

This is what makes spiritual intelligence not only the most mature approach to handling the full spectrum of life's challenges but, again, a genuine career superpower. When you can look at another person, regardless of what they've done, and meet the Truth of who they are with the Truth of who you are, then you can no longer be controlled by your fear. And all you have to do to get there is simply ask yourself, "Am I willing to see the innocence in myself and this person right now?"

Looking at sin

I know. At this point you might be thinking, *wait a minute.* That's fine for an unruly board member, but what about murderers, rapists, traffickers, terrorists, and pedophiles? Are we just supposed to bring those crimes "to the light" and let people off the hook because we all share the same spiritual presence of Love? It's a good question and obviously it's an important one, so, while it may at first seem like a diversion from careers, I want to answer it here within the framework of the *Course.*

Essentially, when we hear about horrific acts like murder and rape, we tend to think of these things as "sin" and, if you come from a traditionally religious background, you've most likely been taught that sin is punishable by "death." As you've probably come to expect by now, the *Course* takes a different approach.

In the *Course*, sin is defined very simply as a "lack of love." (T-1. IV.3:1) That means neither sin nor death can occur at the level of spirit because, again, spirit IS Love and cannot attack, nor can it die. Therefore, "to sin would be to violate reality" (T-19.II.2:2) and this is impossible.

If sin is real, God must be at war with Himself. He must be split, and torn between good and evil; partially sane and partially insane.

(T-19.III.6:3–4)

The point here is that God, being Love, could not have created sin because that would have meant *creating a force that opposes Love.* (As we've already covered, this is also why there's no "devil" in the *Course.*)

What this means is that, in order for sin to be real, it would have to be a power greater than Love.

> **If sin is real, it must forever be beyond the hope of healing. For there would be a power beyond God's, capable of making another will that could attack His Will and overcome it . . .**
>
> (T-19.III.8:1–2)

This goes back to what we've been covering throughout this book regarding spiritual perfection and the illusion of separation. From a *Course* perspective, remember: there aren't "good" and "evil" forces clashing in the universe. There's just God. What God creates (Love) is real, and nothing else ultimately exists. We *think* evil is real because we see the *effects* of it in the world, but that doesn't make it real in the spiritual sense. This is precisely why the *Course* wants you to look at your beliefs. Because if you just isolate the concept of sin alone—if your belief is that you're a "sinner" and that sin is worthy of death—what motivation would you ever have to bring your darkest thoughts into any form of awareness? Why would you willingly do something if you believe God is going to punish you for it? Moreover, if your belief is that "other" people are sinners, *then how else could you view them except by being hypercritical and afraid?* Either way, the belief in sin is keeping *you* stuck in a cycle of denying or hiding the "evil" in yourself while at the same time actively hunting for it in everyone else.

Only by *looking* will we see how this thought system, rooted in judgment and separation, manifests as attack, drama, and unhappiness in our lives—including how we go about engaging in our career. Accordingly, the *one* shot we have at peace within ourselves and in the world is to interrupt this pattern. This means catching ourselves in fear, separation, and judgment and calling out those thoughts for what they are: false projections of the ego.

No one can do this for you, not even God. *You* have to be the one to say, "This thinking is making me insane, and I don't want it anymore."

And when you do, get ready, because then the true miracles can begin . . .

COURSE WORK The mind-wandering exercise

You are much too tolerant of mind wandering, and are passively condoning your mind's miscreations.

(T-2.VI.4:6)

To surmount the many obstacles to peace we all face each day, it's clear that careful attention to our thoughts is required. Most of us, however, aren't in the habit of doing this, and in fact actively find ways to *avoid* what's happening within our own mind. As an example, how many times would you say you check your phone per day? Recent studies suggest the number for most people is around 150, meaning if we subtract eight hours for sleeping and then do the math, that's just over *nine times per hour* or *more than once every ten minutes*. Clearly, we are distracting ourselves to the extreme, and these distractions, when paired with the speed of our lives, are preventing us from looking at what's truly going on in our head.

In this sense, we are *choosing* our own ignorance—though it can hardly be called bliss. The good news, as we've covered in this section, is that when you begin to understand how the ego works, you begin to understand why we do this. In fact, if you remember nothing else about these first chapters, remember this: if a calm mind is a starting point for returning to the Truth about your Self and doing the work of experiencing peace, *then your ego is going to make sure your mind is never quiet enough to get there*.

This is why coddling our pain (by coddling our judgments and distractions) may feel like a form of power and self-protection when it's really the very thing keeping us locked in fear.

As such, your challenge for today is to look closely and vigilantly at your own mind wandering. At work, for instance, whenever you feel the compulsion to check your phone, take a moment and ask yourself: *Why am I doing this? What am I trying to gain? What am I trying to avoid?* Don't attempt to change your thoughts, and definitely don't judge them. Just notice what's going on with a sense of curiosity and then use the space below to write about your experience. In addition to your phone, what are your other big distractions throughout the day? How are you sabotaging your own efforts toward spiritual and professional growth by getting rid of your own peace? Is there someone in your office whom you "love to hate"? What stories are you telling yourself about them? How are you using these and other distractions to avoid probing deeply into *your own* perceptions and beliefs as the *Course* recommends? Please write what comes to you in the space provided.

KEY QUOTES

- The ego's decisions are always wrong, because they are based on the error they were made to uphold. (T-5.VI.4:2)
- A separated or divided mind *must* be confused. It is necessarily uncertain about what it is. It has to be in conflict because it is out of accord with itself. (T-3.IV.3:4–6)
- The ego will always substitute chaos for meaning, for if separation is salvation, harmony is threat. (T-11.V.13:6)
- Knowledge is always stable, and it is quite evident that you are not. Nevertheless, you are stable as God created you. In this sense, when your behavior is unstable, you are disagreeing with God's idea of your creation. You can do this if you choose, but you would hardly want to do it if you were in your right mind. (T-3.V.3:3–6)
- The secret of salvation is but this: that you are doing this unto yourself. (T-27.VIII.10:1)

Part Two

HIRE YOUR Self

Trials are but lessons that you failed to learn presented once again, so where you made a faulty choice before you now can make a better one, and thus escape all pain that what you chose before has brought to you. In every difficulty, all distress, and each perplexity Christ calls to you and gently says, "My brother, choose again."

(T-31.VIII.3:1–2)

The ego's opposite in every way—in origin, effect and consequence—we call a miracle.

(C-2.5:1)

WHAT IS A MIRACLE?

You may be wondering what beliefs around God or sin or separation have to do with the specifics of your own career. After all, how do any of these connect to making more money, acing performance reviews, getting promoted, or leading your teams? The answer to this question becomes clearer when you recognize that everything you do *on* the job stems from the mindset you bring *to* the job. Where the *Course* comes in is that it reminds you just how much the thinking you bring to work each day has been shaped solely by physical sight, and how much this has cost you in terms of your own peace and joy.

Indeed, we all know that every single day our eyes take in the observable part of our experience. We see separate bodies. We see behaviors and actions that are both positive and not so positive. We see work plans, deadlines, and a never-ending stream of emails. This is not surprising. What *is* surprising is how often we forget that what is visible remains *all* the eyes can see.

And yet . . . there's clearly a lot more going on.

From body-identification to spirit-identification

This is why it's dangerous to form your perception of any situation from physical sight alone. We've taught ourselves to believe that our eyes give us the full picture of truth when they really only give us a fraction of it—and even that is subject to our own ego biases and past conditioning. Since leadership and professionalism require a deep level of *un*biased composure and presence, is it any wonder that so many of us are missing the mark?

You believe that what your physical eyes cannot see does not exist. This leads to a denial of spiritual sight.

(T-1.I.22:2–3)

In the *Course* you are asked repeatedly to augment your physical sight with spiritual vision, which requires seeing beyond the limitations of what your eyes are showing you. This shift in perception from "body-identification to spirit-identification" (T-1.I.29:3) *is* the miracle, and since spirit equals Love, this means choosing to perceive with Love.

If you feel some resistance to using the word *love* in a business context, my hope is that Jo's story from the last chapter (as well as other stories peppered throughout this book) can provide some insight into how this particular kind of spiritual intelligence can work "miracles" in your own career, even in highly pressured, fractious circumstances. These are examples of spiritual Love as a source of your power at work; however, it's important to note that, from a *Course* perspective, Love is not just *a* source of power—*it's the only power that exists at all.*

This means that when you choose to see the world from the perspective of your ego (meaning when you choose to see others as separate from you and competing against you) the price you pay according to the *Course* is a total forfeiture of your wisdom and compassion, which is to say a total forfeiture of your power.

***You cannot see both worlds,* for each of them involves a different kind of seeing, and depends on what you cherish. The sight of one is possible because you denied the other.**

(T-13.VII.2:2–3)

Translation: you can't have it both ways. You can't choose the ego and experience peace, compassion, wisdom, or joy at the same time. They simply will not share the same space in your mind. That said, the good news is that when you do make a decision to choose Love, the ego disappears in that moment. Hence, the purpose of a miracle isn't to do anything other than *undo* your belief in the ego's game of projection and specialness, and when this happens, your real power (the Love underneath) is free to emerge and express itself. As always, it's not that the Love wasn't there before. It's only that your experience of it was blocked by your own fear-based thinking.

Remember this from chapter 1?

> God *is*.
> The *is* is Love.
> Love is *all* there is.

Again, the phrase "God is" reflects the idea that the presence of Love is in and around all things (including you) and seeks to express itself through all things (including you). But here's the catch: whether you allow it is a choice. You have to say yes. And the way you say yes to the presence of Love is by letting go of the egoic thinking that blocks it from becoming manifest.

This is why Love cannot transform your career until it first transforms you. As you become more willing to release the ego, this will naturally lead to acting with more inclusion and connection, thus attracting more collaboration with those around you. On the other hand, holding on to the ego leads to acting from a place of scarcity, thus causing more competition and division. Accordingly, if you want to be a leader at work, and if you define leadership as the ability to inspire the actions of other people, then ask yourself, what is more inspiring: Love or fear? The answer is obvious, yet far too many professionals get this backward. They want to be leaders, but egoic thinking causes them to behave in fear-based ways that no one in their right mind would follow.

But that's the whole point, isn't it? We're *not* in our right minds, which explains why we continue to have so much toxicity at work in the first place.

Only Love is real

Returning to the metaphysics, if God *is*, the *is* is *Love*, and we are not separate from Love, then only Love can be real. What this means is that if the ego reflects perceptions of fear and separation, and if perceptions aren't real, *then the ego itself can't be real.* A reflection of nothing is still nothing.

> **And how else can one dispel illusions except by looking at them directly, without protecting them? Be not afraid, therefore, for what you will be looking at is the source of fear, and you are beginning to learn that fear is not real.**
>
> **(T-11.V.2:2–3)**

As I mentioned before, the *effects* of our ego thinking are real enough because we see them everywhere. All you have to do is glance at a newspaper, at your own office, or in the mirror to witness the consequences that fear, projections, and power struggles have in our lives every day. But, again, behaviors are the result of perception, so if you want to change the behavior, you must first change the perception. *This* is the level where the ego isn't real because perception is merely a thought in your mind, and the mind is where you still have the power to choose.

FIGURE 2

Whether you see this apple as red, green, or gray is proof of your mind's ability to choose your thoughts.

To illustrate this idea, imagine that you are holding a green apple right now. See the apple clearly in your hand and perhaps even cup your fingers a bit to mirror its round shape. Now switch the color of the apple from green to red. You can even picture yourself holding the apple while your mind turns the color from red back to green and from green back to red. The simple fact that you can do this is testament to the power you have to choose what you think, and since everything you experience is affected by what you decide to perceive, the goal of the miracle is to bring you back to this decision. In other words, if ego thinking is pushing fear *out* of your mind through projection, *the miracle is pulling it back where you can dissolve the fear by gently choosing against it.*

Love is the highest perception possible

As an example, I'm reminded of my friend Rob (not his real name) who works in an accounting firm where he has an assistant to help with client proposals. Despite the fact that this assistant is supposed to be a full-time employee, she is constantly calling in late for one reason or another and, on a few occasions, she hasn't showed up in the office at all, despite being scheduled for meetings she had agreed to attend.

"At first I tried to be very patient and understanding," said Rob. "I would empathize with her reasons for being late or skipping out, but I would also ask for a heads-up the next time. She'd agree, but then she'd stroll in at ten a.m. like it was nothing on mornings when she had committed to being there by eight-thirty to help with a project."

After his attempts to communicate directly didn't work out, Rob met with the director of human resources (who was technically the assistant's supervisor) to inform him of the situation.

"I was assured the HR director was going to have a conversation with her, but nothing changed," Rob told me. "It got to the point where I stopped giving her assignments altogether. She'd be late getting them back to me, which made me late delivering them to the partners. It was starting to affect my credibility so I just decided to do them all myself."

As Rob's frustration with the assistant grew, he went out of his way to avoid her in the office, but he also began to publicly criticize the management team for not doing more to address the problem.

Rob's breaking point came on a day when he was feeling the pressure of having two proposals due at once. Without a better option, he asked for help from the assistant. As he entered her office to go over some edits, however, she quickly minimized a game on her screen and pulled up the proposal document as if she'd been working on it the whole time. Rob could immediately feel his contempt surging as he turned around and left without saying a word. He then spent the rest of the day and the better part of the evening fuming to anyone in his path.

So where is the miracle in this situation? Communicating with the assistant directly didn't work. Taking the issue to the supervisor didn't work. Telling the partners didn't work. Even his attempts at soft coaching didn't work. Rob had exhausted all the so-called "proper channels" and still . . . nothing.

While he wasn't a *Course* student, I'd had enough conversations about spiritual intelligence with Rob that he was able to recognize—for the first time—that his resentment toward another person was actually hurting himself. When things were going well for him at work, this idea was little more than an abstract notion shared over a cup of coffee, but now that he was actually *feeling* the way his judgment attached him to an experience of suffering, he was ready to learn more.

As we began to talk about Rob's own obstacles to peace, I told him that the *Course* compares grudges to being a prison guard with no more freedom than the prisoner he watches. While the guard may appear to be free, as long as he believes the prisoner is guilty, he'll be forced to stand vigil over the cell, lest the prisoner go unpunished.

**A jailer is not free, for he is bound together with his prisoner.
He must be sure that he does not escape,
and so he spends his time in keeping watch on him.**

(W-P1.192.8:3–4)

Again, Rob understood that his judgment of the assistant was making him unhappy, but this illustration helped him understand why. The real issue was that he felt she was getting away with doing less than everyone else, so he not only had to "keep watch" over his own grievances, but he also had to make sure everyone else knew about them as well. The problem, however, was that it wasn't working. *Her* behavior didn't change while *his* increasing outbursts were starting to make him look like a loose cannon in the office.

There is no order of difficulty in miracles

Having exhausted all his own ideas, Rob was at last open to a miracle—which is to say he was open to viewing the assistant from a place of spiritual vision versus physical sight alone. I started by having him write the first three sentences of the *Course* on an index card and tape it below his computer where he would see it throughout the day. The card read:

There is no order of difficulty in miracles. One is not "harder" or "bigger" than another. They are all the same.

(T-1.I.1:1-3)

Every time Rob looked at the card he was reminded that, since miracles are thoughts of Love and all thoughts are in the mind, he had the power to choose wisdom and compassion at any moment. He was also reminded that the anger he felt was just a thought—no bigger than any other thought and no more difficult to change than imagining a green apple versus a red one.

Eventually, as Rob stopped taking his ego thoughts so seriously, he began to understand that even though *what* he saw didn't change, *how* he saw it could be completely transformed.

Today, Rob continues to work with the assistant (albeit still as little as possible) although her behaviors don't affect him as much as they used to. Instead of getting angry, he silently acknowledges the Changeless within her while focusing on his own projects, which has helped in melting away the emotional baggage that was so heavy in him before. While Rob will eagerly voice his concerns about the assistant to the management team when it feels appropriate, he no longer complains *about* the management to his peers, which he recognized was only going to hurt his chances of moving up in the long run.

What I love about this story is that, since Rob didn't have any organizational authority over the assistant, he was forced to come back to the only thing he could effectively manage in the situation: *himself.* Rob's experience (along with countless other examples) reminds us that sometimes work really isn't fair. Sometimes you'd never hire, much less continue to employ, the people around you and, yes, if you were in charge, things would be run very, very differently.

And yet, says the *Course*, miracles are still possible even in the midst of all that you can't control, and, in fact, if they are *not* occurring, "something has gone wrong." (T-1.I.6:2)

In other words, since peace is your natural state, if you're not at peace, then look no further than the ego to discover where you're blocked. Again, while the ego wants to push your fear out and make something or someone else responsible for it, the miracle brings the fear back into your mind where you can simply let it go. Regardless of what's happening externally, *this is the transcendent power available to you at all times.* And when you begin to experience this power through miracles of your own, as you'll learn in the next chapter, eventually it will become clear that you're not creating them alone.

COURSE WORK The fifty miracle principles

Miracles arise from a mind that is ready for them.

(T-1.III.7:1)

Since a miracle in the *Course* is defined as a shift in perspective from fear to Love, to help facilitate this shift, please read the fifty miracle principles in chapter 1, section 1 of the *Course* text. Read them once as they are written and then slowly read through each principle again, replacing the word "miracle" with "thoughts of Love." For example, in principle 15, the *Course* states: "Each day should be devoted to miracles." (T-1.I.15:1) See how the sentence changes for you when you read it as, "Each day should be devoted to thoughts of Love."

That said, don't spend too much time trying to understand the exact meaning of each principle at this point. Instead, take what you've learned so far and begin thinking about how to apply it to your career. For example:

- In what ways can you use miracle-minded thinking to create an environment where you're proud to work?

- In what ways have you participated in creating an environment where you're not proud to work?

- Where can you bring your own transcendent power to circumstances outside of your direct control?

- Is there any situation where you now recognize yourself as caught in ego thinking?

- What will you do differently if you experience something similar in the future?

You don't have to answer all these questions, of course, but it would be helpful to take a few moments to write about anything that stands out to you in the space provided.

KEY QUOTES

- Miracles are thoughts. Thoughts can represent the lower or bodily level of experience, or the higher or spiritual level of experience. (T-1.I.12:1–2)

- For you can see the body without help, but do not understand how to behold a world apart from it. It is your world that salvation will undo, and let you see another world your eyes could never find. (T-31.VI.3:3–4)

- Corrective learning always begins with the awakening of spirit, and the turning away from the belief in physical sight. This often entails fear, because you are afraid of what your spiritual sight will show you. (T-2.V.7:1–2)

- You see the flesh or recognize the spirit. There is no compromise between the two. If one is real the other must be false, for what is real denies its opposite. (T-31.VI.1:1–3)

- Your distorted perceptions produce a dense cover over miracle impulses, making it hard for them to reach your own awareness. (T-1.VII.1:1)

- Whatever lies you may believe are of no concern to the miracle, which can heal any of them with equal ease. (T-2.I.5:1)

This is a course in
how to know yourself.
You have taught what
you are, but have not let
what you are teach you.

(T-16.III.4:1–2)

MEET YOUR NEW MENTOR

I don't know who sent that press release," said the county commission president, "but whoever it was needs to be fired."

I was twenty-three years old when I saw this quote on the front page of our local newspaper—and immediately I could feel my heart pounding out of my chest.

He was talking about me.

It had been less than twenty-four hours since I had incorrectly broadcast to dozens of media outlets that our state senator had endorsed a controversial project—which he hadn't—and in that time I'd managed to offend the senator, our client, and, evidently, the entire county commission. Needless to say, my morning was not going well.

Still staring at the paper in disbelief, I was jolted by the ring of my desk phone and cringed to discover the blinking light signaled it was coming from Skip, my boss at the time.

"Good morning," I said, trying to sound cheerful.

The response was brief and to the point.

"Got a second?"

As I approached his office wondering how many boxes I would need to pack up my desk, Skip invited me in without any pleasantries or small talk and pointed to a chair in the middle of the room. I sat down like a kid in front of the principal, avoiding all eye contact and bracing for the worst.

"You've really stepped in it," he said, "but I support you, and we're going to get through this."

It's been sixteen years since that meeting, and this story still makes me smile. Not only because Skip was (and still is) an amazing mentor, but because this was one of the first moments when I really "got" the importance of having an advocate on the job. Skip was an owner in the agency where we worked, and this role meant he was included in any closed-door meetings where the future of my career was discussed. I needed him to be on my side, and he was.

My experience with Skip is an example of how employees who find themselves under the wing of a quality mentor tend to go much further faster in their careers than those who navigate their path alone. In this case (and, admittedly, a few others) Skip not only shielded me from the effects of my rookie mistakes, but beyond that, he also taught me the foundational skills of what it means to be a professional. As I've since learned in years of working with executives at all levels, whether a career is built on rock or sand often comes down to who is exposed to these skills—and these relationships—and who isn't.

This makes finding the right mentor at work extremely important, but for so many professionals it just doesn't happen. There are a lot of reasons for this, not the least of which being that there's a certain chemistry that comes with meaningful partnerships that's either there or it isn't. And because you can't fake connection, locating a mentor can often appear as much a game of chance as it is a game of strategy.

Career mentors are very similar to spiritual mentors in this regard. Even a cursory look at the spirituality industry confirms that we are on a multibillion-dollar quest for any course, guru, or temple that promises an experience of divine connection. We call this "being a seeker" and, believe me, I've seen a lot of it. As someone who regularly speaks on career success *and* spiritual intelligence, I've met roomfuls of people who feel abandoned on both fronts, and I understand the disappointment that comes with longing for a guide who never seems to show. That said, the difference between a career mentor and a spiritual mentor is that when it comes to spiritual seeking, we're searching for something that's already ours. From a *Course* perspective, you never have to worry about "finding" a mentor because you've had one all along: an inner guide who couldn't be more perfect for you.

The "Spirit" of spiritual intelligence

To unpack this idea, if you aren't separate from Love (as it says repeatedly in the *Course*), then this means there is a Presence in your mind that is still connected to the Source of all life. The *Course* calls this the *Holy Spirit*, although it also uses other names for this Presence, including Inner Teacher, Voice for God, Helper, Interpreter, Comforter, Universal Inspiration, Mediator, and Jesus. Regardless of the language you use, the definition is still the same: the Holy Spirit is not only your "remaining Communication Link" (C-6.3:1) to spiritual Love, but it's also your way *out* of the ego's thought system.

You cannot be your guide to miracles,
for it is you who made them necessary.

(T-14.XI.7:1)

This is where we have to expand on the definition of *miracles* offered in the last chapter. While a miracle is indeed a "thought of love," in the *Course* a miracle is a thought of love that comes *to* you, and ultimately works *through* you, from the *Source* of Love, which is God. In other words, you can't heal yourself. Presumably you know this already because if you *could* get rid of the anxiety, unhappiness, and fear that accompany ego-based thinking, you surely would have done it already. Still, it should come as a relief to know that the peace and presence you're looking for aren't the result of brainpower or willpower but, rather, about *willingness* to invite a Wisdom greater than your own into your decision making.

Along that line, this is also where we have to expand on our definition of *spiritual intelligence* from chapter 1, because if you'll recall, in that chapter I noted that spiritual intelligence is commonly described as "*the ability to behave with wisdom and compassion, while maintaining inner and outer peace, regardless of the situation.*"[1] This is certainly true; however, what's implied yet unsaid here is that "acting with wisdom and compassion" (i.e., Love) is the *effect* of tapping into this Inner Wisdom. It's the "Spirit" that makes spiritual intelligence spiritual; otherwise there would be very little to distinguish it from emotional intelligence or even mindfulness.

This is an important contrast to make, particularly in business settings, where the word "spirit" is so controversial that it tends to get diluted into broader terms like "purpose" and "values." (I should know, by the way. I've been teaching spiritual principles—while calling them values—to corporate audiences for years.) Still, while I believe employers are wise to keep religion out of the office, in your own mind it's important to know that you have a *spiritual* mentor who can help you in all aspects of your life at all times. Thus far, I've been calling this mentor your Higher Self, but to be clear, what we're talking about here is the Holy Spirit.

Defining the undefinable

Before we go further into what the Holy Spirit can do for your career, I think it would be helpful to understand a bit more about what the *Course* says the Holy Spirit *is*. The simplest way to explain a very big concept is to note that, since we've fallen asleep to our spiritual sameness, the purpose of the Holy Spirit is to help us wake up. In other words, if the ego is a thought of separation leading to fear, the Holy Spirit is a thought of connectedness that brings us back to Love.

To open the eyes of the blind is the Holy Spirit's mission, for He knows that they have not lost their vision, but merely sleep.

(T-12.VI.4:2)

As such, it's important to understand that, according to the *Course*, when you call upon the Holy Spirit you're not trying to invoke anything that's outside you. Spiritually speaking, there's nothing "out there" to connect with anyway. You are simply reaching into the part of your mind that *is* the Love beyond the limitations of your egoic perceptions and small, separate self. This is why you don't "find" Love but, rather, you bring it. *How else would love enter a room if not through you?* Thus, the more you know yourself as Love, the more you strengthen the bond with your own inner mentor and grow your capacity to become a mentor to others who are long-starved for exemplars of grace in business.

Connecting to your career mentor

If you have been searching for both your inner spiritual mentor and external work mentors with little success, the good news is that while these relationships are obviously very different in form, in content they flourish in similar ways. Namely, you begin slowly and grow over time with a steady stream of little right actions.

As an example, let's think about how you would go about finding a mentor in your career. To begin, you'd most likely identify someone who has been where you want to go and then reach out to establish a connection. Being the smart person you are, you wouldn't ask him or her for any favors up front. Instead, you'd give first by contributing to a project they're working on, sharing articles of interest, or just passing along a few well-timed, sincere compliments.

After you've gotten to the point where the other person recognizes your name (at the very least), perhaps you wade in a little further by asking a simple question and seeing how enthusiastic they are in helping you answer it. Assuming the response is positive, let's pretend this opens the door to a brief meeting or phone call.

This is excellent progress, right? Your preferred mentor has agreed to chat with you.

At this point you have two options when it comes to how to handle the next step. You can view it as a basic get-to-know-you session and arrive with no plan *or* you can come with a clear intention to deepen the relationship. Maybe you bring an idea to the table that you feel is relevant to their business, maybe you bring a professional challenge and ask their advice, or maybe you even bring both. Regardless, the point is that you've done some homework that not only gives the conversation some scaffolding, but also demonstrates that you have a genuine respect for the other person's expertise and busy schedule.

Which strategy do you think is going to work best when it comes to developing a relationship over the long term? Clearly it's the planned approach, and yet I can't tell you how many professionals I've met who simply wing it in meetings with potential mentors. They approach big opportunities like these hoping for a positive outcome and then get sorely disappointed when the connection either doesn't materialize at all or fizzles out quickly. These are often the same professionals who expect the *mentor* to manage the relationship, realizing far too late that the mentor's contribution is traditionally their time and expertise, while it's generally the *mentee*'s job to initiate communication and handle any logistics involved.

Connecting to your inner mentor

Understanding the process of how to nurture a mentoring relationship at work has many parallels to nurturing a relationship with your inner mentor. For starters, you wouldn't approach a career mentor if he or she hadn't achieved something that you want for yourself. This does not mean you seek connections that are purely transactional, but it *is* what makes a mentoring relationship different from, say, a friendship. In other words, there's a give-and-take that is related to the mutual goal of professional growth.

In the case of your inner mentor, the goal is growth as well, but the way of getting there is very different. The Holy Spirit doesn't guide you to receive what you've made special in the world, but rather, it restores your spiritual vision and thus guides you to transcend the world. To be sure, just as you wouldn't ask a restaurant manager for advice on how to be an attorney, you'll be setting yourself up for disappointment if you ask your inner mentor for advice on how to get external things. This, by the way, explains why even our most sincere requests (i.e., our prayers) often appear to be ignored. We're asking for *specifics*—"Give me this thing that I want"—and Spirit is patiently waiting for us to ask for the one thing it can provide: *a miracle*.

What this means is that in the *Course*, the Holy Spirit is far more interested in healing your mind than in changing the circumstances of your life, and responds to requests only at the level of thought. But here's the key: the miracle IS what ultimately changes your life. Since "you cannot behave appropriately until you perceive correctly" (T-1.III.6:5), this means when your thoughts are in alignment with Love, you'll automatically know the action to take that would be in your best interest overall.

Bringing your spiritual mentor to work

Imagine the impact that connecting to—and trusting—your inner guidance would have on your career. For starters, it would mean that, regardless of the situation you're facing, you would no longer have to worry or wonder about what to "do." Instead, you would focus your attention on *how to think* and, the more you think with a miracle-minded perspective, the more you'll discover that this creates better outcomes for everyone.

As an example, consider for a moment the difference in energy you'd bring to a meeting where you *had* to get a certain result versus the energy you'd bring if your intention was simply to be helpful and of service. In the first scenario, your angsty vibe would most likely prevent you from getting what you want. On the other hand, if you shift your focus from managing the outcome to managing your own perception, then not only does this open your mind to possibilities you wouldn't have considered otherwise, but people will be more willing to collaborate with you *because* they know you're not trying to manipulate them. This isn't to say that you don't ask for what you want; the key is to be clear on *where you're coming from when you ask*. When the goal is to align your perspective with Love, the *effect* is that you act with greater wisdom and compassion. This makes you extremely impressive—particularly under pressure—without your having to strive to be impressive at all.

Accordingly, whenever you'd like to engage your own inner guidance at work—before an important meeting or an interview, for example—bear in mind this key similarity between career mentors and your internal mentor: in both situations *you* are the driver of the relationship. In the office, it's your job to go to your mentor when you need help versus hoping they will automatically know when to swoop in and save the day. From a spiritual perspective, the parallel here is that you not only have to be clear on what you're asking for—meaning a shift in perspective leading to more loving behavior—but in order to get it you have to ask, *period.*

The Holy Spirit cannot speak to an unwelcoming host, because He will not be heard.

(T-11.II.5:1)

Listening to Spirit vs. ego

Now let's go further into what happens when you decide to call upon the inner guidance referenced in the *Course* as the Holy Spirit. By this point I'm going to assume that you're on board with the idea that underneath those layers upon layers of judgment, specialness, and projections, we all have a peaceful Presence within, leading us to "a better way."

Now what?

While the *Course* doesn't use this language, it does state that the sole purpose of the Holy Spirit is to shine as a lighthouse in our mind, guiding us back to Love. Or, to put it another way, since we all have thoughts of fear (the ego), thoughts of Love (the miracle), and the ability to choose between them, the Holy Spirit serves as a gentle reminder that Love is the only choice that will allow us to experience a sense of peace.

The Voice of the Holy Spirit does not command, because It is incapable of arrogance. It does not demand, because It does not seek control. It does not overcome, because It does not attack. It merely reminds. It is compelling only because of what It reminds you *of.* It brings to your mind the other way, remaining quiet even in the midst of the turmoil you may make.

(T-5.II.7:1–6)

When it comes to the Holy Spirit, however, the bad news is that we're often too distracted, too mentally cluttered, and, frankly, too captivated by the very thinking that blocks our ability to hear it. Hence, the more static the ego creates in our mind, the less we are able to tune in to the inner mentor that is our only way out. Compounding this problem is the fact that the ego "always speaks first" (T-6.IV.I:2), which means that any time you are taking steps toward a more connected and loving perspective, *the ego will be there immediately*, tempting you to believe that you are alone and unworthy of Love and success in any form.

In addition, as you pay attention to your ego more carefully, over time you will also notice that not only does it tend to be the *first* thought you hear, but it also tends to be the *loudest*. This is to be expected, although what you shouldn't expect is that the Voice of the Holy Spirit will become louder to compete.

Pain is not of Him, for He knows no attack and His peace surrounds you silently. God is very quiet, for there is no conflict in Him.

(T-11.III.1:5–6)

And so here we come to another famous *Course* query: How do you know when you're listening to the Voice of the Holy Spirit versus the ego? I doubt there has ever been a *Course* student who has not asked themselves this at some point, so it's likely that when you start turning toward your own inner guidance to help with challenges in the workplace, the question will come up for you too. As such, it's immensely helpful that the *Course* is clear on the answer.

The *Course* says the ego always speaks first and that it's wrong. In order to hear our inner guidance we must quiet our minds, be willing to let go of any investment in the answer and listen to that still, small voice within us. The fact that our inner guidance is never strident, but speaks to us in a peaceful, loving voice, is a sign of its authenticity, and I think all of us have to learn with practice to make that distinction.

WILLIAM THETFORD, COAUTHOR, *A COURSE IN MIRACLES*

As Bill said, once you understand what you're looking for, it becomes very easy to tell which voice you are hearing, and with practice, this ability only becomes stronger over time. Simply put, if you hear a thought of judgment, separation, blame, or shame in any form, it's the ego. If you hear a thought of healing or connection, it's the Holy Spirit. You can also tell which voice you're listening to by how it makes you feel as a result. If a thought causes you to feel anxious or tight in the chest, you can be sure it's the ego. On the other hand, if you feel relaxed and warm, this is Spirit. As Bill mentioned as well, since the Holy Spirit whispers and is unconcerned with form, if the *tone* of the voice is overly loud or overly specific, this is also a sign of egoic thinking.

Remember, though, that despite the fact that the ego can cause a tremendous amount of suffering and despite the fact that it *feels* like it's coming from "you," at the end of the day, *it is nothing*. Again, the ego isn't an entity or an external force of its own. It's a thought—and a thought by itself is no more powerful than a shadow on the sidewalk. It's only our *investment* in thoughts that turns them into beliefs. Therefore, keep in mind that the ego isn't something to be afraid of; it's something only to be dismissed. With the help of your inner mentor, you *can* fire the ego as your teacher and, as you'll learn in the next chapter, you can do it this instant.

COURSE WORK Listening to the Holy Spirit

If you cannot hear the Voice for God, it is because you do not choose to listen. That you *do* listen to the voice of your ego is demonstrated by your attitudes, your feelings and your behavior.

(T-4.IV.1:1–2)

Today your miracles-at-work challenge is to practice listening to the Voice of the Holy Spirit. Again, if you prefer not to use this language, that's perfectly fine. Just substitute words that are more meaningful to you (e.g., listening to love or listening to your inner guide) and apply the same process. Also, since this exercise works nicely as a meditation, I've created the following step-by-step outline for your reference, as well as an audio version that can be downloaded at miraclesatworkbook.com. Please note that you can do this exercise anywhere, including at your desk, and you are invited to keep the practice going for as long as you find it helpful.

1. To begin, please sit in a comfortable position and close your eyes. Take three deep breaths, inhaling through your nose and exhaling through your mouth, and then sit for a few additional moments of uninterrupted silence.

2. Notice any resistance you have around the concept of an inner spiritual guide. Notice whether this resistance comes in the form of judgment, feelings of doubt or disbelief, a sense of unworthiness ("Who am I that Spirit would speak to me?"), anger, hurt, or any other thoughts of separation that will block your ability to hear.

3. With your eyes still closed, repeat the following sentence (inspired by workbook lesson 254) at least three times, either out loud or in your mind, while placing both hands on your chest above your heart.

   Let every voice but Love be still in me.

4. Keeping your spine tall, your eyes closed, and your hands over your heart, sit in silence for the amount of time that feels meaningful to you, always staying connected to your own heartbeat. As you listen for the Holy Spirit, remember that you are not asking to hear something specific about what to do at this point. You are asking for guidance in *how to think* with Love.

5. Slowly come out of your meditation by taking another deep breath, saying "thank you" at the top of your inhale and again at the bottom of your exhale. Continue these breaths of gratitude as you wish—inhale *thank you*, exhale *thank you*—and when you're ready, gently open your eyes.

To deepen your practice of communicating with the Holy Spirit, I recommend you read workbook lesson 221 in the *Course* upon waking in the morning and at night before you go to sleep; do this for as long as you find it helpful. Repeat the title of the lesson slowly a few times—*peace to my mind, let all my thoughts be still*—and just listen. If you don't "hear" anything at first, don't worry. Just stay focused on what you feel instead. Keep repeating these steps as needed until you begin to develop a stronger sense of love for yourself, your inner guide, and all beings—remembering that the sincerity you bring to the process means far more than getting the steps or the words perfect. As the *Course* says repeatedly, you cannot fail at this because the Holy Spirit "will respond fully to your slightest invitation" (T-5.VII.6:6), meaning that no request for healed perception ever goes unanswered.

KEY QUOTES

- You cannot see the Holy Spirit, but you can see His manifestations. And unless you do, you will not realize He is there. Miracles are His witnesses, and speak for His Presence. (T-12.VII.4:1-3)

- Truth can only be experienced. It cannot be described and it cannot be explained. (T-8.VI.9:8–9)

- Miracles demonstrate that learning has occurred under the right guidance, for learning is invisible and what has been learned can be recognized only by its results. (T-12.VII.1:1)

- . . . you must look in before you look out. As you look in, you choose the guide for seeing. And then you look out and behold his witnesses. This is why you find what you seek. (T-12.VII.7:1-4)

- Judgment you taught yourself; vision is learned from Him Who would undo your teaching. (T-20.VII.8:4)

- "Who walks with me?" This question should be asked a thousand times a day, till certainty has ended doubting and established peace. (W-pI.156.8:1–2)

If you are tempted to
be dispirited by thinking
how long it would take
to change your mind so
completely, ask yourself,
"How long is an instant?"

(T-15.I.11:1)

THE HOLY INSTANT

Mitchell was the owner of a floral delivery service with five locations throughout two states. In just under a decade he had turned a small loan from his parents into a multimillion-dollar business, although with big growth came big expenses, and he occasionally struggled to make payroll.

Tammy had worked for Mitchell since the very beginning and was the first employee he hired when the company started to take off. Barely out of college when she joined the team, Tammy had proven herself to be smart and dependable so Mitchell kept giving her more responsibilities until she essentially ran all the day-to-day operations. Despite the financial stresses, Mitchell and Tammy had always worked well together—that is, until one day when things stopped being so rosy.

It began on a morning when Mitchell was driving to work and received a call from an old friend and client. After catching up on an order scheduled for that afternoon, Mitchell casually mentioned that he hoped his friend enjoyed the gift card he had given him for being such a loyal customer.

"I'm not sure what you're talking about," said the friend, "but if you want to give me free money I'll take it any day."

Mitchell laughed, but at the same time he felt a sudden pang of anxiety.

Something wasn't right.

When Mitchell arrived at the shop, he asked Tammy about the gift card and she told him she had sent it to the customer the week before. Mitchell didn't probe any further, in part because he really wanted to believe her. A few phone calls later, however, and his worst suspicions were confirmed.

Credit card statements showed that $2,000 in gift cards had been purchased, yet *none* of the eligible clients Mitchell called had received one. When he confronted Tammy with this information, she confessed that she'd been stealing the cards for months. After all they had been through together, and especially since she knew how much every dollar mattered, it's safe to say that Mitchell was devastated.

What do you do when someone you trust lets you down? What is the miracle-minded perspective when your pain is bigger than words and you're left picking up the pieces of a relationship that will never be the same?

In Mitchell's case, he wanted to send a "strong" message to Tammy and the rest of the staff, so his way of handling the situation was to fire her on the spot, in front of everyone, in no uncertain terms. As you might expect, this is hardly a show of strength from a *Course* perspective.

After he let Tammy go, Mitchell wanted to stop replaying their confrontation over and over in his head, and the fact that he couldn't only made him more angry. He started to have difficulty sleeping and, while he had always been somewhat impatient, his mood swings got worse and seemed to last for days at a time.

"Why am I being the one tortured here?" he asked. "She's the one who committed a crime. Shouldn't *she* be the one to pay for it?"

Insane premise = insane conclusion

When you've been wronged by the actions of another person, an understanding of the obstacles to peace (discussed in chapter 4) becomes essential. In other words, it's important to recognize that you're not actually "losing" your composure, *you're giving it away* in every moment you see yourself as the innocent victim of someone else's betrayal. As it says in the *Course*:

> **Anger cannot occur unless you believe that you have been attacked, that your attack is justified in return, and that you are in no way responsible for it. Given these three wholly irrational premises, the equally irrational conclusion that a brother is worthy of attack**

rather than love must follow. What can be expected from insane premises except an insane conclusion?

(T-6.IN.1:3–5)

In a mind where fear has hardened into anger, it's practically impossible to stop ruminating over a hurtful situation regardless of how hard you try. This is a state where you *believe you've been attacked*, which typically causes you to counterattack (if "only" in your head) while at the same time believing that the results of your attack aren't your fault. As we've covered, this is the attack/defense cycle that creates the "insane conclusions"—the pain of life—until the pain eventually takes over and the cycle starts again.

Of course, the real "insane premise" the *Course* is referring to here is that you could ever be attacked at the level of spirit. Yes, your body is vulnerable to attack (both physical and emotional), *but you are not your body*. This is what you must acknowledge to reclaim the peace and sense of power that allows you to choose Love over fear. Knowing that you are far more than just a body is the first step to knowing that when you ask for a miracle from the Holy Spirit (by whatever name you call it), what you are really asking for is to recognize this Truth about yourself and everyone else.

Enlightenment is but a recognition, not a change at all.

(W-P1.188.1:4)

Simply put, your release from fear isn't about praying for the situation or the other person to change. Again, it's about recognizing that which cannot change. This means praying to see through the ego's projections, separation, and specialness within your own mind, and when this happens—even if only for a moment—the *Course* refers to it as a *holy instant*.

What is the holy instant?

To understand what the holy instant is, you must first understand what you are. As such, *the* crossroad question on your *Course* journey is this: Do you believe that you are a perfectly whole extension of Love, eternally one with All that is, or do you believe that you are a body, separated and vulnerable to the attacks of other bodies? Again, if you believe that Love is perfect and exists in you, then from a *Course* perspective it *has* to exist perfectly in everyone or else it *couldn't* exist in you. As we covered in the first chapter of this book, perfect *in one* means perfect *in all.*

But forget not that my faith must be perfect in all your brothers as it is in you, or it would be a limited gift in you.

(T-15.VI.2:4)

The holy instant is nothing more—nor less—than knowing this is true. It's a moment that happens both in time and yet beyond time because you're not filtering your perception through what occurred in the past or what you expect to happen in the future. You are simply using your spiritual vision, with the help of the Holy Spirit, to see the perfection in All that is present right now, *in this instant.*

There is no past in the present

Remember how your feelings and actions are driven by the meaning you give your experience? *Where do you think this meaning comes from?* If the ego is in charge, you can bet the biggest part of it is rooted in the past.

Touching back on Mitchell's story, this is why he *still* gets annoyed when Tammy's name is mentioned, despite the fact that it's been years since he let her go. Note the classic ego patterns of specialness, projection, and "Self" sabotage here. By isolating Tammy for her behavior in the past and then making her the target of his "special hate" in the present, Mitchell is ensuring that nothing will change in the future. He will continue to be upset—with all the unfortunate side effects of choosing to enshrine his negative energy—and he won't know that his own thinking is the cause.

The holy instant is an admission that this doesn't work.

When your peace is threatened or disturbed in any way, say to yourself: I do not know what anything, including this, means. And so I do not know how to respond to it. And I will not use my own past learning as the light to guide me now.

(T-14.XI.6:6-9)

In the *Course*, by not using "past learning" as your guide, the warning is to not use *the ego* as your guide. And yet, if "your peace is threatened" in the first place, this is a sign that you're *already* in the ego's territory, and probably because, like Mitchell, you've brought something from the past into the present and given it the power to hurt you here and now.

Therefore, when you say, "*I do not know what anything, including this, means*," the idea is that you no longer choose to rely on your own judgment in the situation, and this is what opens you to guidance. The importance of this step cannot be overemphasized because when you ask for a holy instant—which, again, the *Course* says you must do in order to receive one—*you won't be able to hear the answer if you think you already know what it is*. Just this single act of accepting that you don't know what is best, as opposed to stubbornly insisting you do, is all you need to create the tiniest crack of space in your mind. And yet, this is all the space you need to choose a new teacher.

What happens in a holy instant?

Let's say someone you work with has let you down. You've asked for a miracle, meaning you've asked to receive a cleansed perspective in the form of a holy instant, and now you're sitting at your desk with one question in mind.

What happens next?

If you're expecting an immediate, cloud-parting moment of insight, you'll probably be disappointed. I'm not denying that can happen; it's just never been my experience or that of any of my *Course* groups. Rather, what typically occurs after asking for a holy instant is . . . *nothing*. You carry on as usual, the only difference being that you're not imposing your will by anxiously stewing about the future or replaying different "what if" scenarios in your head. *You are simply open to the mystery*. You've sent a prayer to the universe, and how quickly you receive a response to this prayer—whether it takes a minute, an hour, a day, or even weeks—depends on how willing you are to get out of your own way. That said, as a general rule, you'll know a holy instant has arrived when three things come into focus: (1) you recognize that the cause of your suffering is not the other person or their behavior but in your own ego thinking, (2) the ego is merely a lack of love, and (3) the remedy is forgiveness.[1]

Since we've already covered the first two, it's now time to tackle *the* cornerstone of the *Course*, namely its radical reframe on the topic of forgiveness.

What is forgiveness in the *Course*?

When you hear the word *forgiveness*, what is the first thing that comes to your mind? For many, it's a gesture of grace shown by one person to another who has insulted or abused them. While this is the world's definition of forgiveness, in the *Course* this is actually another form of separation (meaning it's another way to rank ourselves as "more than" or "less than"), which makes it yet another form of ego attack. In fact, the very notion of forgiving someone simply because you're attempting to be "charitable" or "letting them off the hook" is what the *Course* unpleasantly labels *forgiveness-to-destroy*.

> **. . . there are the forms in which a "better" person deigns to stoop to save a "baser" one from what he truly is. Forgiveness here rests on an attitude of gracious lordliness so far from love that arrogance could never be dislodged. Who can forgive and yet despise?**
>
> (S-2.II.2:1–3)

Pay close attention to the language here: the "gracious lordliness" needed to "stoop" down and "save" another person from knowing "what he truly is" is "arrogance" so cleverly disguised that it's perceived as "love." What this means is that true forgiveness in the

Course is *not* seeing the other person as "wrong but forgiven" (which implies that you are "right" and therefore "better") but, rather, it's knowing that the sacred essence of who they are is *always* right.

Obviously this is difficult, particularly when you really do feel violated or betrayed by someone else—*which is exactly why you need help*. The lower self can't reach this level of forgiveness on its own, in large part because the lower self *is* the ego and the ego needs conflict to survive. Thus, by asking for a miracle, what you are really asking for is the spiritual vision required not just to forgive the behavior, but to suspend judgment entirely.

This is where forgiveness emerges as less of a nice thing to do in order to prove to yourself and everyone else how gracious you are, and more of a requirement for *your own* happiness and the retention of *your own* power. In other words, you cannot be truly happy or composed unless you're at peace, and you cannot be at peace unless you forgive.

Think of this like a circle with the Higher Self/Holy Spirit in the middle and all the ego's thoughts around the edge. The more you focus

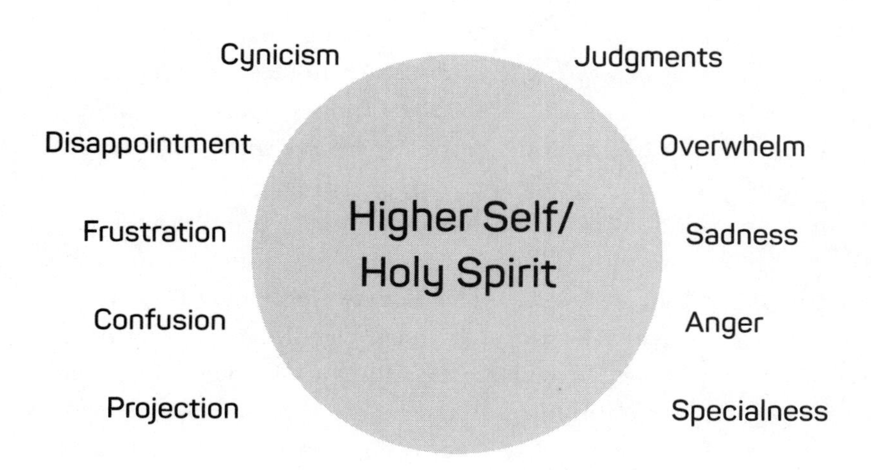

FIGURE 3
The Higher Self/Holy Spirit amid a selection of the ego's trappings.

on the hub at the center, the more you are thinking in alignment with Love, resulting in behaviors that reflect wisdom and compassion. On the other hand, the more you allow your thoughts to drift to the outer rim, the less you are thinking with Love, resulting in less connection and greater fear. *Which do you think is going to make you more effective at work?*

Returning to Mitchell, how do you think he would have behaved differently if he had taken the time to ask for a miracle, choosing to see Tammy as her Highest Self, before he met with her? Yes, he would still have to let her go and, yes, he could even file charges, but imagine how much better things could have gone if Mitchell hadn't approached the whole situation while completely lost in the rim of his ego? Imagine if he took a moment in advance to say, "*I do not know what anything, including this, means,*" and left room for Love to enter versus believing his anger was "strength" and allowing it to consume his whole being?

Mitchell assumed that spiritual intelligence, and the notion of forgiveness in particular, would make him look "weak," and yet his story exposes how ego thinking is the real weakness. In the *Course*'s version of forgiveness, what you're doing isn't a form of complacency or allowance. Asking for a miracle through a holy instant does not mean that you won't take action when needed; it only means that *when* you take action it will come from a place of recognition that the other person is, at the deepest level, one with you. You can do this without coddling them or dropping all boundaries. (In fact, you don't even need to physically *see* the other person in order to turn over your anger and judgment *about* them, which, again, you must do for your own sake.) This is why forgiveness isn't about avoiding or denying the fact that you've experienced a truly painful situation. It's about denying the situation any power to affect how you choose to lead yourself and others. *This hardly makes you a doormat.* As you can see, it is your source of strength because it separates you from the compulsiveness that tends to make things worse in the long run.

Taking your power back

It's very easy to get caught in believing that your challenges are resolved only when the outcome you want is achieved (e.g., *When* this person is gone, *then* I'll be happy), but again, this only keeps your power outside of your direct control. The *real* power comes from knowing you don't need external conditions to be a certain way in order to show up as your best. If you think it would take a miracle to practice this consistently, you're absolutely right. The whole point of the *Course* is that it *does* take a miracle, and the holy instant is what happens when you ask for one.

In the last chapter, I noted that it's comforting to think of a miracle as the moment when the Holy Spirit comes swooping in to solve all your problems; however, it's important to remember that you're not getting a genie here. You're getting an answer to your call to replace egoic thoughts of judgment, attack, and separation with thoughts of Love. As such, the request isn't, "*Please make sure I never experience this anger again*," but rather, "*Please help me reorganize my thoughts of anger so that I am able to see this person differently*." It's a subtle distinction but an important one because the goal isn't to remove all ego thoughts of separation or judgment entirely. That's certainly a noble objective, but it's just not a very practical one for our purposes. Instead, the goal is to have no ego thoughts "that you would keep." (T-15.IV.9:2) And, as always, you'll know when you're holding on to ego thinking when you lose your sense of peace.

* * *

So, as a quick recap, when you're caught in the rim of the ego's thought patterns, sooner or later this will ripple out into your behavior and obviously affect your results. Therefore, if you want your *results* to be better, this means you have to follow the trail back to the source (your thoughts) and ask for a miracle (a shift in your perspective) that will enable you to forgive (the holy instant). In the *Course* the Holy Spirit is your "Helper" in this process, but make no mistake: you're doing much of the heavy lifting by noticing those moments when you are slipping into fear, asking for help, and being open to the guidance you receive.

That said, there will be plenty of times when you screw this up. There will be times when you send the email you should never have sent, say the thing you should never have said, and behave in ways that make it hard for you to forgive yourself. In these situations, you're no longer spinning over what someone else has done, but what *you* did in reaction to it . . . and the guilt is thick. Clearly, it's time to choose again.

In the *Course*, the practice of unwinding any ego-based decisions you have made is called *the atonement*. In the atonement you are asked, first and foremost, to reflect on your own thinking and return to "the point at which the error was made." (T-5.VII.6:5) Since an "error" in the *Course* equals a lack of Love, this means you are asked to return your mind to the moment when you allowed the ego to take over. In other words, the moment when you had a decision to make between Love and fear . . . and you chose fear.

Next, the *Course* suggests that you "atone" for this error by turning it over with the following prayer:

I must have decided wrongly, because I am not at peace.
I made the decision myself, but I can also decide otherwise.
I want to decide otherwise, because I want to be at peace.
I do not feel guilty, because the Holy Spirit will undo all the consequences of my wrong decision if I will let Him.
I choose to let Him, by allowing Him to decide for God for me.

(T-5.VII.6:7–11)

The more you practice forgiving yourself and others through the process of the holy instant and the atonement, the more you will discover that the burdens of guilt and shame will lift, taking with them all that stands between you and healed perception. Thus, when the mind is swept of all ego-based debris, as you'll learn in the next chapter, you become ready to step into your true purpose, at work and in the world.

COURSE WORK The habit of forgiveness

Do you want a quietness that cannot be disturbed, a gentleness that never can be hurt, a deep, abiding comfort, and a rest so perfect it can never be upset? All this forgiveness offers you, and more.

(W-P1.122.1:6 / W-P1.122.2:1)

Lesson 122 of the *Course* workbook is titled "Forgiveness offers everything I want." For today's miracles-at-work practice, we are going to test this assertion by making forgiveness a daily habit. There's no pen or journal required for this exercise and it shouldn't take more than three to five minutes at a time. In fact, the only thing you need to get started is to simply ask yourself two questions in the evening before you go to bed: *Who have I not forgiven?* and *What do I need to let go of?*

As thoughts of specific individuals and situations arise in your mind, remember that when we talk about forgiveness in the *Course*, the idea is not to overlook issues that need to be addressed. The point is to correct your perception so you are able to see the Perfect in all, even through actions that are frequently imperfect.

Look on your brother with this hope in you, and you will understand he could not make an error that could change the truth in him.

(T-30.VI.10:1)

If you look at the sentence above closely, you'll notice that "understanding" comes after "hope." This is important to recognize because it means that when you come into this practice with a willingness to see the truth, *vision will be given to you*. And so, by taking this time to ask yourself these questions in a "mini-atonement" session at the end of the day, you may not understand *how* it happens, but you will know true forgiveness when you feel it. And that will be enough to know that Love is Real.

KEY QUOTES

- The holy instant is the Holy Spirit's most useful learning device for teaching you love's meaning. For its purpose is to suspend judgment entirely. (T-15.V.1:1–2)

- When you feel the holiness of your relationship is threatened by anything, stop instantly and offer the Holy Spirit your willingness, in spite of fear, to let Him exchange this instant for the holy one that you would rather have. He will never fail in this. (T-18.V.6:1–2)

- If you remember the past as you look upon your brother, you will be unable to perceive the reality that is now. (T-13.VI.1:7)

- In the holy instant nothing happens that has not always been. Only the veil that has been drawn across reality is lifted. Nothing has changed. (T-15.VI.6:1–3)

- You who want peace can find it only by complete forgiveness. (T-1.VI.1:1)

- There is no false appearance but will fade, if you request a miracle instead. (T-30.VIII.6:5)

As an expression of what you truly are, the miracle places the mind in a state of grace. The mind then naturally welcomes the Host within and the stranger without. When you bring in the stranger, he becomes your brother.

(T-1.III.7:4–6)

YOUR PRIMARY FUNCTION

Maybe by now you've noticed that the *Course* makes some fairly bold claims about the nature of reality. After all, it's asking you to believe that the definition of God is the all-encompassing presence of Love, that suffering is the result of forgetting your connection to this Love, and that healing occurs with a shift in perception granted by the Holy Spirit upon your request.

It's a lot to take in, I know.

Therefore, let's suspend *Course* theology for a moment and consider a practical career question: *What kind of professional do you want to be?* If you're reading a book like this, it's safe to assume that you want to do more than just cope with your job. Presumably your goal is to move up, which will eventually require taking on greater leadership roles.

This brings us back to the discussion around behaviors *worth following*, as well as to the question of whether being manipulated by egoic thoughts and emotion is compatible with garnering influence. We all know the answer to that, and yet when it comes to the deep presence needed to inspire and motivate others, it seems even the best intentions often break down under the multitude of triggers that pop up during an average workday:

Interpersonal problems

Deadlines and performance pressure

Unaccountable teammates

Feeling powerless to affect change

Feeling disrespected

Feeling ignored

Feeling overwhelmed

Job loss

Role confusion

Evaluations

Personal or health problems impacting performance

Ethical dilemmas

Organizational restructuring, etc.

Reduced to their most basic level, each of these triggers—and the countless others just like them—represents an opportunity to choose how you will perceive and respond, a choice the *Course* describes as one between "littleness and magnitude." (T-15.III) As it says in the text:

> **Every decision you make stems from what you think you are, and represents the value that you put upon yourself. Believe the little can content you, and by limiting yourself you will not be satisfied.**
>
> **(T-15.III.3:3–4)**

Just think about that for a moment: *Every decision you make stems from what you think you are.*

Essentially, the *Course* has always presented this to you as a choice between "littleness" (ego) and "magnitude" (Love), and thus far I've tried to outline its case for why choosing littleness is directly tied to every form of unhappiness and career implosion.

This is why the principle of atonement, introduced in the last chapter, is so vitally important to the practice of the *Course*. Specifically, it represents the moment when you get to *choose again*. The atonement is when you remember your Magnitude, regardless of your circumstances, and it's from this miracle-minded perspective that true leadership emerges. Indeed, the actions you take from knowing your true Self are the highest peak—and the highest reward—of spiritual intelligence.

Even so, we don't tend to look at our lives in a miracle-minded way. Quite the opposite, actually. We usually examine our circumstances first *and then* determine our capacity for leadership based on whether we believe we're facing a "big" issue or a "small" one. *But what problem could you possibly face that is any bigger than the Magnitude alive in you?*

Therefore, instead of seeing the world through the filter of your challenges and hoping to find the Magnitude at the center, the *Course* is asking you to see the world through your Magnitude, which allows you to meet any uncertainty of life with certainty of Spirit.

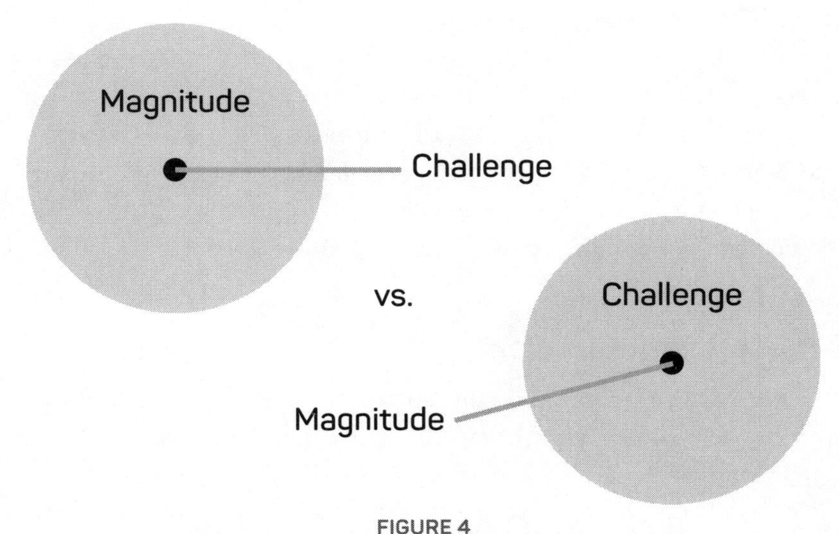

FIGURE 4
When faced with a challenge, which do you see first: the depth of the problem or the depth of your Magnitude?

This is when spiritual intelligence becomes far more than just a tool for professional growth; it becomes a fundamental change in your entire worldview. In short, when you know that *you are Magnitude itself*, you access a "stately calm within" (T-18.I.8:2) so powerful that any littleness attempting to break it can only break itself against it.

As such, your primary function from a *Course* perspective is not to search for your Magnitude—because you never lost it. Rather, your function is to seek out the *littleness* within your thinking and atone for it by asking for a miracle and then simply making another choice.

All striving must be directed against littleness, for it does require vigilance to protect your magnitude in this world.

(T-15.III.4:4)

With the ego out of the way, the Love and Magnitude of your Higher Self will naturally shine through in your behavior. This is why the *Course* says the "sole responsibility" of the miracle worker is to "accept the Atonement for himself." (T-2.V.5:1) By accepting the atonement—meaning by turning your thoughts back to an awareness of interbeing—you are not only addressing the problem where it can be fixed (your mind), but you are also providing a demonstration to other people of the power within themselves. Simply put, as *your* thoughts are healed, you automatically develop the ability to heal others by your example of true Magnitude at work.

Your primary function

This is why your most important job, regardless of what your business card says, is to *be the light* that shines away the darkness of the ego. Your "profession," as the *Course* calls it (T-1.III.1.10), is to embody the Magnitude that is your "natural inheritance" (T-In.), and the way to do that is to remove the littleness in your own mind through moment-by-moment forgiveness.

I am the light of the world.
That is my only function.
That is why I am here.

(W-PI.61.5:3–5)

Accordingly, what would it look like if your goal each day were simply to be a light in your office? How would you carry yourself differently if you truly believed that forgiveness is your *first* job and everything else is secondary? How would you treat your colleagues if, from the moment you open your eyes in the morning until the moment you close them at night, your core belief is that you and everyone else around you are a holy home to Magnitude itself?

If you think that sounds naïve, let's consider how it stacks up when compared to the kind of professional you aspire to be. In my courses, I've asked hundreds of executives to complete a freewriting exercise describing a leader they deeply respect and why. Given that we tend to admire others for the qualities we'd like to embody ourselves, the end result of this process is to identify these qualities and develop action steps around them.

As you'd expect, some remarkable discussions about what it means to be a great leader have emerged from these courses, and I can say that, without exception, everyone identified as worthy of deep respect was recognized because they were authentically in their Magnitude. This is not the language that is typically used, of course, yet the *effect* is exactly the same. As always, it's about the energy and presence that naturally come forth when your mind is in alignment with Love. As an example, here's an excerpt from a recent workshop participant who described her former supervisor. (Please note this was pulled from a freewrite, which is basically a stream of consciousness on the page.)

> Just being around him is transformative—he is the embodiment of true kindness and yet he's not afraid to make tough decisions. He's attentive with a sense of humor, aware of himself and others, dignity, calm, focused, joyful, authentic, free-spirited, comfortable in

> his own skin, doesn't take himself too seriously, humble, deeply patient, and also filled with a quiet confidence and a deep understanding and patience for what it means to be a human being and the nature of the human mind. He speaks slowly and carefully, and never seems as if he has somewhere else he needs to be.

Far from being naïve, I would argue that this is actually the most sophisticated way you can show up in the world. *Who wouldn't want to work with or, better yet, **be** this kind of leader?*

Becoming a leader of Magnitude

So now the question becomes, what does it take to be a leader of Magnitude? In the *Course*, the key is to "hold your magnitude in perfect awareness" (T-15.III.4:5), which means to see with spiritual vision *first* and physical sight second. This is why you need a moment-by-moment practice of forgiveness. It's *forgiveness*, through the holy instant and atonement, that returns your perspective to Love and allows you to see the divinity in humanity. As you may know, this is what we mean when we use the word *namaste*, which loosely translates to "I bow to the divine in you" or "the divine in me salutes the divine in you." It's vitally important that you understand this definition of forgiveness or you will misunderstand both Magnitude and your function.

For instance, if you understand your function is to "be the light" *without* understanding this particular context of Magnitude, you might simply assume the goal is to shower other people with affection. While this can be described as a form of love, it's the wrong target for our purposes because it's clearly inappropriate in a business setting.

Accordingly, you'll be relieved to know that fulfilling your function of Love does not mean running around your office in a cloying state of sweetness. This book contains many stories highlighting the fact that you don't even need to *like* someone in order to recognize the Sacred in them, which is important to note since you'll always find yourself working with people you'd never hang around with otherwise. That said, the point the *Course* is making here is that the best way to demonstrate Love is by *vigilantly rejecting all that is not Love*. Or, to put it another way, the awareness of Magnitude comes through the release of littleness—and the release of littleness comes through a practice of forgiveness. While the *Course* doesn't present this process as a linear or step-by-step path, hopefully by now you're getting a sense that there is actually an order emerging based on what we've covered thus far.

> **Magnitude** is the presence of holy Love in and around all living things.
>
> **Ego thinking** is what blocks your awareness of this Love.
>
> **Atonement** is the moment you see a choice between Love and fear (the ego) and you choose Love.
>
> **Prayer** is a request for spiritual Vision over your own limited perceptions.
>
> **The holy instant** is the result of your prayer when Love becomes fully accessible to you.
>
> **Forgiveness** is the result of the holy instant when you see the Magnitude of others beyond any bodily or personality differences.
>
> **A miracle** is the result of forgiveness when your perspective is healed by returning to Love, thus allowing Love to work through you.
>
> **Special function** is a call to extend the miracle of your healed perspective to others.

As you can see, there's a lot more that goes into receiving a miracle than just saying a prayer and waiting for the *aha* moment. In fact, even when the *aha* moment arrives—meaning when you feel the sense of peace that comes from atonement and forgiveness—your "job" still isn't done. It's not enough to experience the miracle for yourself and simply stop there. To "be the light" is to shine brightly by showing others a better way. As always, you don't have to mention any of these ideas to colleagues and, frankly, it would probably be better if you didn't. Sharing (or "extending" as the *Course* calls it) only means that, as *you* live from these principles, you demonstrate what the *Course* calls "standing for the alternative." (M-5.III.2:6)

A stand for Magnitude

My favorite example of this concept in action occurred recently during a career workshop hosted by Marianne Williamson. In the Q&A session, a woman who looked to be in her mid-forties stood up and began to tearfully relay a heartbreaking series of life misfortunes. Dead-end job. Abusive husband. No money to feed her children. As each setback became more distressing than the last, everyone sat in pin-drop silence, and it was clear that her suffering was deeply felt around the room. "I just don't know," the woman concluded, "what else to do."

After listening intently, Marianne took a brief pause to collect her thoughts and then replied softly, "That is an incredible story, and I'll bet you get a lot of attention for it. But I'm just not going to go there with you." The words were delivered with an appropriate level of compassion, but they hung in the air with unmistakable resolution.

This is "standing for the alternative" as the *Course* describes it. All the woman saw in herself was littleness while all Marianne saw in her was Magnitude. Body-identification versus spirit-identification. Moreover, by gently calling out this woman on her attraction to pain, Marianne not only named a key block to her power, but she also named how those of us in the audience were unintentionally reinforcing her victim perception by leaning in with our "you-poor-thing" faces.

To empathize does not mean to join in suffering, for that is what you must *refuse* to understand. This is the ego's interpretation of empathy, and it is always used to form a special relationship in which the suffering is shared.

(T-16.I.1:1–2)

Until Marianne broke the spell (so to speak), the room was heavy with what we assumed was empathy when all we were really doing was "joining in suffering." To the *Course*'s point, this is the ego's version of empathy because it doesn't free the other person from fear; rather, it *strengthens* the fear that keeps *everyone* stuck as a result.

Think about those times in your own career when someone has approached you with a problem and, instead of modeling the Highest Self in action, you sunk into the littleness. We've all been there, whether it's piling on to office gossip or taking sides in a petty argument, and yet by being "little" ourselves, we've not only denied *our* Magnitude, but we've denied someone else the opportunity to see theirs as well.

This is why you don't want to make an idol of your own suffering, nor do you want to give others permission to do so in your presence. For far too long our struggles have been used not as bridges to higher ground but as ladders on which to erect identities of misery. Unfortunately, we then have a tendency to stand back and marvel at the pain, while the bridge to growth remains unnoticed and uncrossed.

Needless to say, there is a distinction to be made between a healthy analysis of problems as a way to avoid future missteps and an unhealthy fixation on suffering as an excuse to stay small. Only you can know which is true for you, but returning to the woman in Marianne's workshop, it was clear that she had been carrying the albatross of littleness for years and it was time to change the story.

Marianne, by holding a vision of her Magnitude, was essentially saying, "Regardless of how you see yourself, I will see the Truth of who you are and I will be your eyes until you come around." It was an unforgettable moment, not only because this woman was finally able to catch a glimpse of her full potential at last, but because her respect for Marianne motivated her to embody it. Again, this is Love according to the *Course*, but there's another word for it as well: this is *leadership*.

Indeed, if you want to be a leader of significance, a leader whom people will write about as someone who truly inspires them—then hold a space to see others in full Magnitude until their vision catches up to your own. You cannot do this if you are harboring judgments, idolizing problems, comparing, or encouraging others to do the same. Your pity and insecurities are a gift to no one. Only your Magnitude, strengthened through forgiveness, is a gift to all because it is the light that will guide you and everyone else home. This is your primary function, and those around you who are blind to themselves are desperately waiting for you to claim it.

COURSE WORK **Attuning to your purpose**

Workbook lesson 64 states: "Only by fulfilling the function given you by God will you be happy." (W-pI.64.4:1) Since the *Course* says that our function is to demonstrate *Love*, this sentence can also be read as: "Only by *Love* will you be happy." Seems true enough, right? I'm sure if you were to think about the times in your life when you experienced the most joy, chances are you would find those were moments spent doing something you love or being surrounded by people you love. But now let's think about "Love" as it's defined in this chapter.

Because if you view Love as abandoning all that is *not* Love, then the sentence above can be read a little differently. Now it can be interpreted as: "Only by *releasing littleness* will you be happy." From a *Course* perspective, all three of these statements are true, but being mindful of how you respond to each of them is a worthy experiment. How does it feel to think of "Love" at work as rejecting littleness? What would that even look like to you? For instance, do you get overly defensive when challenged? Are you determined to win even the most trivial of disagreements? Do you carry around grudges for months? If you can develop the self-awareness to notice "little" behaviors that are blocking the full expression of your Magnitude (or blocking you from seeing the Magnitude of others), then you have a much better chance than you would have otherwise of dissolving them before they become "big."

To do this, whenever you feel agitated or troubled in any way, the *Course* recommends asking yourself one simple question:

> **This is the question that *you* must learn to ask in connection with everything. What is the purpose? Whatever it is, it will direct your efforts automatically.**
>
> (T-4.V.6:8–10)

Accordingly, your miracles-at-work challenge for today is to keep this question—What is the purpose?—at the forefront of your mind. You can write it on your hand, write it on a sticky note, or set it as a reminder on your phone; anything works as long as it's something you will see multiple times throughout the day. The point is to use this question as a reframe to consider the ultimate objective of your thoughts and, consequently, your behaviors.

As an example, if you suddenly feel the urge to send a heated message, by asking, "What is the purpose?" you'll create a speed bump in your mind to explore whether your goal is to understand another person's point of view or whether it's to highlight how badly they are wrong. As Marshall Rosenberg, founder of the Center for Nonviolent Communication, used to say, "Connection comes before correction." In other words, when your purpose is connection, the right solution will always present itself.

KEY QUOTES

- A holy relationship starts from a different premise. Each one has looked within and seen no lack. Accepting his completion, he would extend it by joining with another, whole as himself. He sees no difference between these selves, for differences are only of the body. (T-22.In.3:1–4)

- Choose littleness and you will not have peace, for you have judged yourself unworthy of it. (T-15.III.2:2)

- Your practice must therefore rest upon your willingness to let all littleness go. (T-15.IV.2:1)

- And while you fail to teach what you have learned, salvation waits and darkness holds the world in grim imprisonment. (W-pI.153.11:3)

When a brother
behaves insanely,
you can heal him
only by perceiving
the sanity in him.

(T-9.III.5:1)

THE DEFENSELESS DEFENSE

Elaine had been working with her colleague and close friend Donna for almost six months to plan an important training rollout for their company. It was a meeting open to senior management only, so Elaine viewed it as a chance to make a good impression and, hopefully, a springboard to larger opportunities.

Cut to the morning of the event when Elaine and Donna are reviewing the agenda with their managing partner to brief him on the day ahead.

"After the keynote I'm going to announce the winners of the door prize," said Elaine, "and then we'll break for lunch."

"Wait a second," said Donna. "I thought we were going to do the door prize at the end of the day because we didn't think there would be enough time before lunch?"

Elaine could feel herself getting slightly annoyed, not only because they had discussed the timing of the door prize at least twice before, but also because she felt second-guessed in front of their supervisor, who was now staring at both of them with a look of confusion.

What Elaine didn't know at the time was that this was the first of *many* wrinkles Donna would add to her day. Regardless of who was around, Donna questioned Elaine's decisions on everything from seating arrangements and parking validations to speaker selection and even gift-bag distribution. No issue, it seemed, was too large or too small for her critique.

Elaine was surprised and disappointed by this behavior because she believed Donna should have pulled her aside to raise objections and because she felt most of Donna's concerns had already been addressed in the planning process. It was not only time-consuming to have to go back and rehash the same discussions on-site, but Elaine felt it made both of them look unprepared and unprofessional. Eventually, about six hours into the event, the last shred of Elaine's patience broke.

"Could you *please* stop telling me how to do my job?!" she snapped.

Elaine immediately regretted both her words and her tone, but by the time she could apologize, Donna had already walked off in a huff. As if that wasn't bad enough, Elaine turned around and noticed that three of her colleagues—including her boss—had witnessed the whole thing.

Above the battlefield

What do you do when your Magnitude completely dissolves into littleness? What happens when you had every *intention* of "being the light" but you feel like the cord got ripped from the wall before you had a chance to turn on the lamp? These are important questions at any stage of your career but they are especially critical in leadership roles, given that you can't expect others to embody their Highest Selves at work if you aren't embodying yours.

From a *Course* perspective, the thing to remember here is that while disagreements are normal, *conflict* is the ego's playground. The *Course* even says that the ego "becomes strong in strife" (T-5.III.8:8), which means that when you allow a situation to escalate to the point of aggression, you are empowering your own fear *and* demonstrating fear-based behavior to others. This not only keeps *you* in "hell," but it also takes everyone else down with you.

As such, consider this for a moment: When your ideas and opinions are challenged in the office, how would you describe your default response? Personally, I've never known anyone who confessed to enjoying drama, but I certainly know enough people who do their best to attract it. I also know people (myself included at times) who are like Elaine in the sense that they don't seek friction but they can be baited into it or, at the very least, have the potential to make a situation worse than it needs to be.

Naturally, there are many different approaches to handling conflict at work, and for years we've been offered well-meaning advice on the "best" ones to choose. Depending on the situation, we are told to back down and save our bullets for more consequential fights, or we are told to double down, or we are told to settle. All of these strategies have their place, but they also come from a perspective of being "on the battleground," as the *Course* describes it. In other words, if you are looking at conflict through the eyes of the ego alone, then *because* you see everyone as separate, they have to lose in order for you to "win." (Even a compromise means that someone has to give up something.) This cycle of compete-to-defeat is how we've been trained to view winning in practically every aspect of life, including our own companies, where the message on success is often loud and clear: *to be the best, you have to beat the best.*

Again, if you had no exposure to the ideas presented in the *Course*, it would be very easy to assume that the way to win any conflict is by *attacking* another person's position and *defending* yourself against their attacks on you. This is arguably the most common approach to disputes, yet it's clearly not the most enlightened one for our purposes because it's essentially trying to eliminate the ego by using the ego. As the *Course* says, "Do not think that fear is the escape from fear." (W-pI.170.9:1)

This is why whenever you do get pulled into littleness, it invariably has an effect that is completely counter to what you originally intended. In other words, the attack/defense cycle masquerades as the *escape* from fear—no one can touch you if you're "strong," right?—when all it really does is *reinforce* the fear.

In the story above, for instance, Elaine was trying to make Donna more compliant, but she actually made her more resistant. Moreover, Elaine was afraid Donna's questioning would hurt her reputation as someone of high potential, but in raising her voice—and getting caught by her boss—she wound up damaging the very thing she was trying to protect. Going back to Mitchell in chapter 8, his attempt to demonstrate authority merely exposed his insecurity, and on and on it goes.

What if instead of trying to win on the battlefield, we left the battlefield altogether?

Remembering your Magnitude

This is where understanding the concept of Magnitude becomes very important. Simply put, when you know that your Magnitude cannot be threatened, you know that winning the ego's battles means you stop fighting them. Yes, you'll still stand up for what you want and believe, but the difference now is that you no longer find value in attack as a way to get it.

The strong do not attack because they see no need to do so. Before the idea of attack can enter your mind, you must have perceived yourself as weak.

(T-12.V.1:2–3)

Physical sight alone will tell you that you can be weakened, and indeed, the ego is very good at keeping score of battles you've "won" and "lost." Spiritual vision, on the other hand, sees that any clash of personality has no effect on the Truth. You are not the self who can be hurt by the actions of another; you are the One who is aware of the self who feels the hurt, yet exists in a state of Grace beyond it. The Love that you are doesn't share in your judgments and fragmented perceptions about yourself and those around you. Rather, your Magnitude "stands radiant, apart from conflict, untouched and quiet" (T-23.I.7:10)—and this is the Source of your strength. Anything else, the *Course* says, is "a war of two illusions" in a "state where nothing happens." (T-23.I.7:8)

Still, when you are unaware of your Magnitude, this is when you deflect Love and enter the battlefield. Your fearful thoughts cause you to behave in ways that are unloving, which then results in others being unloving toward you, so you become even more unloving toward them, and the vicious circle continues. *Is engaging in pettiness what you want to be known for at work? Is this the kind of thinking you want to bring to your toughest career challenges?*

In the last chapter you were encouraged to interrupt ego thinking by asking, "What is the purpose?" as a way of examining your intentions whenever you feel your peace beginning to slip. Accordingly, if your purpose is to meaningfully connect with another person—which you must do to motivate them at work, can you *really* expect to do that when you are attacking them in your mind?

Returning to Elaine, she eventually apologized to Donna for her behavior, blaming her outburst on the stress of managing the event. However, if we look deeper, it's easy to see the real issue was that Elaine chose littleness over Magnitude. Her small self was threatened, and so to avoid feeling helpless, she projected the threat onto Donna. Elaine's purpose was not to connect—it was to win. And what else can come from an ego purpose other than an ego experience?

Until Elaine becomes aware of the fact that her real purpose—her function—is to choose against the ego and, thus, become a clear channel for Love, she will continue to re-create the ego's drama in different forms. Next time her issue may not be the stress of event planning, but it will always be something equally outside of her control so she can be equally blameless for her reaction to it. With so little awareness of the ego's tricks, is it any wonder that they've had so much power over her?

If Elaine had simply paused and asked herself, "What is the purpose of this thinking?" she would have caught her ego's attempts at separation. Next, by asking, "Would I want to have perfect communication, and am I wholly willing to let everything that interferes with it go forever?" (T-15.IV.8:3) she could have avoided the unnecessary spat with Donna in the first place. Note, however, that "perfect communication" in this sense doesn't mean finding the ideal *words* to say. It means establishing an awareness of Magnitude first, *and then* deciding from a miracle-minded perspective what to do next.

Finally, since the *Course* says that "prayer is the medium of miracles" (T-1.I.11:1), if Elaine had asked for help—"I feel myself in judgment, but I am willing to see this differently"—then perhaps her anger would have lifted entirely, or perhaps she would have addressed Donna in a way that didn't leave her feeling belittled. Regardless, Elaine would not have been speaking from an energy of division and anger, and this alone would've increased the odds that she may have actually been heard.

Salvation is a collaborative venture

Given how much the *Course* focuses on interpersonal relationships, it's easy to see why it calls "salvation" a "collaborative venture." (T-4. VI.8:2) As you may have noticed, this is a path where you don't find God by looking *up* at a celestial creator, but by looking *at* the person right in front of you. Seeing the Magnitude in others is what enables you to see your own, which means that *your* healing is directly tied to theirs.

What you perceive in others you are strengthening in yourself.

(T-5.III.9:5)

This is why healing is described in the *Course* as a gift that defies physical law by adding to both the receiver *and* the giver. As a perhaps overly simplistic example, if I have a cookie and I give you half, then technically I have less and you have more. But if I share my healed perspective with you, then by seeing your Truth, I have not only given *you* a gift (a.k.a. a miracle), but I've given myself one too. *My* healing grows as I share my Magnitude, and the same is true for you. *Every* person and *every* encounter, the *Course* says, gives you the opportunity to "find yourself or lose yourself" depending on whether you choose Love or fear as your teacher.

When you meet anyone, remember it is a holy encounter. As you see him you will see yourself. As you treat him you will treat yourself. As you think of him you will think of yourself. Never forget this, for in him you will find yourself or lose yourself.

(T-8.III.4:1–5)

Understanding that every encounter—indeed, every *instant*—has the potential to be holy is not only what allows you to forgive those who have fallen asleep to their Magnitude in your presence, but it's also what allows you to atone for when you fall asleep to your Magnitude in theirs. To visit Elaine and Donna's story again, Donna's actions brought to light something unhealed *in Elaine*; otherwise she wouldn't have gotten so angry. (And vice versa, by the way.) This is why the *Course* says, "In my defenselessness, my safety lies." (W-pI.153) Thus, after the training conference, when Elaine was finally able to drop her ego's defenses—meaning once she stopped blaming Donna and started looking inward—she realized the real trigger wasn't Donna's second-guessing; it was her own feelings of nervousness and self-doubt about the event. Donna's questions merely triggered this fear, causing Elaine to *attack* in order to *defend* herself. This was not only a lousy management strategy, but it left her staring down the barrel of her ego once again.

That evening, however, Elaine did ask for help. She reached out with what the *Course* calls the healer's prayer—*Let me know this brother as I know myself* (T-5.In.3:8)—and she simply got quiet. She replayed the moments leading up to her outburst, moments when she knew she was getting irritated but didn't say anything, and thought about how she could have handled the whole situation differently.

What if, instead of allowing the anger to build and ultimately explode, she had met Donna's escalating anxiety with a sense of curiosity? Rather than giving curt answers to Donna's specific questions, what if she had just taken a few minutes to pause and say, "I'm sensing some uneasiness. Would you like to talk about it?"

Per the *Course*'s practice of atonement, Elaine was particularly interested in finding the point at which she stopped focusing on the event itself and started assigning blame. In other words, *when* did she choose fear?

Elaine approached this process not as a cross-examination against herself but as a prayer and a reflective meditation. She knew she had gotten something wrong because she wasn't at peace, and she genuinely wanted to know what had happened within her own thinking so she could be more mindful the next time. Perhaps she could prevent a similar—or worse—outburst from occurring again.

Only appreciation is an appropriate response to your brother. Gratitude is due him for both his loving thoughts and his appeals for help, for both are capable of bringing love into your awareness if you perceive them truly. And all your sense of strain comes from your attempts not to do just this.

(T-12.I.6:1–3)

At the end of the day, Elaine realized that the exchange between her and Donna had ultimately been a blessing because it allowed her to discover much about herself that would make her a more valuable coworker, leader, and mentor. She also recognized that what she had learned would enable her to communicate better with her husband and her two daughters, and it was *this* that really made her heart swell with gratitude. She had been given an opportunity to *choose again*, and that was something to be thankful for indeed.

COURSE WORK The "no language" experiment

When you recognize what you are and what your brothers are, you will realize that judging them in any way is without meaning. In fact, their meaning is lost to you precisely *because* you are judging them.

(T-3.VI.3:2–3)

When you are in a leadership role, you are a "signal sender," which means that, particularly during times of challenge, others will be looking to your behaviors for clues as to the severity of a situation, as well as for guidance on how to respond. With this in mind, let's consider the kind of signals you are sending at work through your words, your actions, and indeed your very presence.

From a *Course* perspective, if the message you're communicating is anything but joyful, you are denying yourself and others the opportunity to learn what it means to "stand for the alternative" (meaning stand for Love) in this world. In fact, the *Course* even states that your slightest sigh has the potential to "betray the hopes of those who look to you for their release." (W-pI.166.14:1) This means that if you want to send the signals of a composed leader within your organization, you must first be *genuinely* composed yourself.

One exercise that can help in this regard is a mindfulness practice called "no language."

To get started, all you have to do is set an intention to approach each encounter with your colleagues and clients—particularly the ones you find difficult—*without* bringing past judgments into the present. You don't have to do anything outside of your normal routine; the only difference is that as you pass your coworkers in the hall, attend the meeting, or deliver the presentation, you're not thinking about what someone else did five years ago or even five minutes ago. Rather, you are making a sincere effort to see the innocence of everyone you meet by seeing them with "no language"—which really means no *baggage*.

For example, as you arrive at the office in the morning, look your colleagues in the eye and say hello, imagining that you are meeting them for the very first time. Notice what comes up for you around this idea—maybe it's resistance, maybe it's embarrassment, or maybe you even notice some preferential treatment arising because you find it's more comfortable to practice this with some colleagues than it is with others. All of what you're feeling right now just *thinking* about doing this says something about where you're choosing Love and where the ego still has some well-worn grooves in your mind that are worth bringing to light.

As always, this isn't something you need to articulate to anyone, and it's obviously not intended to be used as a way to drop boundaries that have good cause for being there. This is simply an opportunity to notice where you are adding meaning to the facts of what you see and how it's keeping you "on the battlefield" of ego judgments and biases. Try this for at least a full day and write about your experience in the space provided.

KEY QUOTES

- See no one from the battleground, for there you look on him from nowhere. (T-23.IV.7:1)

- Your brother has a changelessness in him beyond appearance and deception, both. It is obscured by changing views of him that you perceive as his reality. (T-30.VIII.2:3–4)

- Stop for a moment now and think of this: Is conflict what you want, or is God's peace the better choice? Which gives you more? A tranquil mind is not a little gift. (M-20.4:6–8)

- If you will recognize that all the attack you perceive is in your own mind and nowhere else, you will at last have placed its source, and where it begins it must end. (T-12:III.10:1)

- However much you wish he be condemned, God is in him. And never will you know He is in you as well while you attack His chosen home, and battle with His host. Regard him gently. Look with loving eyes on him who carries Christ within him, that you may behold his glory and rejoice that Heaven is not separate from you. (T-26.IX.1:3–6)

No one can be untouched
by teaching such as this.

(T-14.V.7:2)

THE GIFT OF JOY

Learning, as we've all experienced, can be painfully incremental. In school, for example, we are exposed to a concept, we study it, we reflect on it, and then (if we're lucky) we retain it just long enough to pass a test. Healing is often viewed as a similarly aggregate process. In other words, it's not enough to attend *one* therapy session, coaching call, or recovery meeting. True headway requires showing up for weeks, months, or even years with discipline and follow-through.

If you look at the journey you're taking with the *Course* as one of healing from the ego, you might be tempted to view it through the same lens of cumulative growth and get discouraged. After all, the ego may be an illusory belief system, but it's one that took years to learn and will surely take years to *unlearn*, right? While that assumption would be true if spiritual growth were bound by time, fortunately for us, it isn't.

I AM is always present tense

The state of grace that is your spiritual home, says the *Course*, is always *now*: a vertical axis of moments where the only thing that binds you to the past or to the future is in your own mind. To unpack this further, if Reality (capital "R") is defined as *now*, and if healing is defined as *a shift in perception*, then where else could a perception shift occur *other* than the present? This is why healing from the ego's fear, depression, and anxiety isn't contingent upon what you have done in the past or what you will do in the future. Your Magnitude doesn't come from achieving something you don't have; it comes from recognizing what you already are. This makes the path of the *Course* nothing more than a moment-by-moment decision to choose the teacher of Love over the teacher of fear, which you can do—*right now*—just as easily as someone who has spent decades studying the finest wisdom of enlightenment.

> **For only "now" is here, and only "now" presents the opportunities for the holy encounters in which salvation can be found.**
>
> (T-13.IV.7:7)

You are, the *Course* says, the holy home of God, and all that stands between you and pure joy is your unwillingness to believe it. In fact, if you *did* believe it, would you so eagerly yearn for the vision board filled with things that will make you happy "someday"? Only by denying your own power could you view the beauty of *this* moment as a mere stepping stone to the next one, and have so little faith that what you don't have is far better than what you do. *Joy* is what arises when these and all other ego obstacles fall away.

Love and joy are one

Indeed, since we've spent a nontrivial amount of time in this book on the topic of Love, it's worth noting as we close that, in the *Course*, Love and joy are exactly the same. Consider the significance of this statement given all that we've learned thus far. Specifically, if our function here is *healing*. . . and if healing is *extending Love* . . . and if Love is *equal to joy*, then this means *joy heals as Love heals*. Going back to the part in the *Course* where it says our function is to be the "light of the world" (W-pI.61.5:3), this can also be interpreted as saying that our function is to be the *joy* of the world.

To repeat: our function is to be the joy of the world.

Assuming we find joy in the same way the *Course* says we find Love, this means that regardless of your job, your main "profession" (T-1.III.1:10) is a moment-by-moment rejection of all that is *not* joy. As with Love, this comes with a daily practice of *forgiveness* toward yourself and others, which builds in you a resilience that is capable of holding the full spectrum of life. By learning to forgive or even, as the *Course* says, *laugh* at the ego's "tiny mad ideas" (T-27.VIII.6:2), over time you discover that your loving, happy, and celebratory moments will be felt more deeply and with more presence, while any negative or unpleasant experiences will be given less weight and emotional attachment.

Every minute and every second gives you a chance to save yourself. Do not lose these chances, not because they will not return, but because delay of joy is needless.

(T-9.VII.1:6–7)

With this in mind, it's worth considering how your day-to-day behaviors at work would pass the following litmus test: *Do your thoughts and actions bring you closer to or farther from joy?* You'll know the answer, by the way, when you consider whether you find yourself moving closer to or farther from loving other people. When you withhold your capacity to give Love, you withhold your capacity to experience joy. It really is as simple as that.

While this could be a barometer for success in all aspects of life, it's particularly essential to your career because there's no teamwork without connection, there's no connection without love, and there's no love without joy. Remember: *every* person you encounter—including those you did not choose to interact with but who show up in the workplace as your boss, employee, peer, or colleague—offers you the opportunity to see the interconnectedness of all things. This is the secret to *your* joy and *your* influence. It may not be the fastest route to the top, but it's the strongest foundation you'll have for the journey by far.

Just think for a moment about what it would mean to build a career in which *joy* is the measure of your success. Clearly, we are more comfortable looking at our jobs through the eyes of fear—Will I have enough money? Am I getting noticed?—but it doesn't have to be that way. The *Course* is gently calling you to recognize that the world can be as easy as knowing you've chosen the ego when you're not at peace and knowing you've chosen Love when you experience joy.

Don't wish for Love. Become it.

If you'll recall from the introduction to this book, part of my motivation for writing about spiritual wisdom was to help coaching clients find an experience of peace through life's most painful events. As it happened, just a few months after I began working on this book, I had a heartbreak of my own in the sudden death of my beloved grandmother, a woman for whom there are no words to fully express my devotion and gratitude.

Anyone who has experienced a loss like this knows that these are the moments when life comes sharply into focus and connection emerges, at last, as all that really matters. The evening before my grandmother passed away, when all the IVs had been removed and the only sound in her hospital room was the steady hum of an oxygen machine, I crawled into her tiny bed and lay beside her for more than an hour. Somehow knowing this would be our final good-bye, I rested my head on her shoulder, put my arms around her waist, and through a river of tears told her how much I loved her.

Where, you may ask, is the peace or the joy in this?

Lying there in a dim room next to my grandmother, staring at the flickering light of a muted television, I thought of the passage from the *Course* I've referred to throughout this book: Nothing real can be threatened and nothing unreal exists. (T-In). It occurred to me that, even though I wouldn't see her here in *form* anymore, the *content* of her love would be available whenever *I* chose to embody and share it. While I would (and do) miss her specifically—yes, I miss *her* eyes, *her* laugh, and *her* hugs—the Love she reflected is still present because *I* carry it. That part of her isn't gone simply because she is, which means that whenever I want to feel a connection to her, all I have to do is bring the expression of Love she represents to others. This is the cycle of interbeing and spiritual intelligence we've been touching upon from the very beginning. It's a Magnitude that is both imminent and transcendent, and you discover it *everywhere* by virtue of the fact that you decide to see it in *everyone*. *I am* my grandmother, and so are you. Not tomorrow. Not six months or a year from now. But right now in this moment. Nothing else exists.

Understanding and demonstrating this same kind of metaphysical Love is not only the way you find the miracle within your own challenges, but it's also the way you "teach" *A Course in Miracles*. This, once again, *is* leadership. As always, it doesn't minimize the gravity of any pain you face, nor does it give you a pass from mourning when appropriate or taking action when needed. That said, it is the perspective that allows you to show up each day offering your gentle smile and stately calm as proof that you cannot be broken—and *this* is the true miracle at work.

Praying for the highest good

I saw this concept in action recently when one of my clients experienced a beautiful moment of strength and leadership amid what was otherwise an extremely stressful situation. This particular client was the vice president of a Fortune 500 company, a job she'd held for ten years with nothing but favorable performance reviews, and yet because of a corporate restructuring she found herself preparing to re-interview for her own position against other candidates. Needless to say she was disappointed; however, she also discovered that she was experiencing a flood of other emotions she found increasingly hard to conceal, including nervousness, bewilderment, and anger.

"I think you should pray," I told her. "But don't pray to keep your job. Pray for the highest good for all involved."

At first my client said this felt a bit too passive, but eventually she realized that what she was really asking for was hardly apathetic or indifferent. *After all, she was asking for a miracle.* Obviously, we could have spent a lot of time tinkering with the externals of her circumstance—role-playing possible interview questions, for instance—and while that was still a good idea, it dealt with her challenge only at the surface level. Consequently, even if everything she said in the interview were to be impeccable, the moment even a hint of contention bubbled underneath her words, everyone would feel it. (This was also true for her more casual interactions in the days leading up to the interview, by the way. If she had allowed her anxiety to leak onto her coworkers, this would have compromised her leadership presence and possibly stained the interview process before it even took place.)

Thus, by "praying for the highest good," my client was able to detach from what she couldn't control (the outcome) and reconnect with what she could: dissolving her own ego thinking. This allowed her to come to the interview far more at ease, which in turn allowed her to think better on the spot—which resulted in her keeping her position.

This is another example of love at work as the *Course* defines it. My client wasn't "being loving" through overt and inauthentic displays of affection to her boss or anyone else. She was being loving by being aware of the thoughts in her mind that reflected littleness and refusing to allow those thoughts to commandeer her behavior. By approaching the interview fully prepared yet with an energy of acceptance, allowance, and, yes, even *joy*, she naturally made herself the most attractive person for the job.

On the surface it may seem as if this story and that of my grandmother's passing have little in common. A deeper examination, however, reveals that they both offer proof that because there is no order of difficulty in miracles, there is no challenge your Magnitude cannot solve.

An invitation to joy

> **We practice coming nearer to the light in us today. We take our wandering thoughts, and gently bring them back to where they fall in line with all the thoughts we share with God. We will not let them stray.**
>
> **(W-PI.188.9:1–3)**

So now it's your turn to come nearer to the light. You have been given practices within these pages to reconnect to the peace that has always been your home. As you apply these ideas to your own life, remember once again that joy is the marker of your success. When you laugh at judgment, you steal its power. When you choose Love, you dissolve the fear. And when you find yourself with wandering thoughts, remember to gently bring them back, knowing that your path to peace is to see the Changeless in all, to walk in the footsteps of forgiveness, and to provide no home for judgment in your mind. *Wouldn't you rather have these principles as your compass?* If you agree, then let your inner guidance be the center of your career and you will experience a sense of wisdom and compassion that can only be described as unshakable. You may not be able to change your circumstances with the snap of your fingers, but you can remember your Magnitude in the middle of *all* that life brings—and be glad. So let this be your *one test*: to find the perfect grace and complete freedom from fear available to you in each moment through your decision to choose Love. Pass this test—if only for an instant—and you have passed this *Course*.

COURSE WORK Miracle Working

. . . what is yours will come to you when you are ready.

(T-24.VII.8:2)

Have you ever noticed how life tends to blow up right before something far greater emerges? At first all you see is the rubble of what was, but when the dust finally clears you realize that whatever you "lost" was merely preventing you from an evolution that will ultimately serve you better. In the Manual for Teachers, the *Course* calls this "a period of undoing." (M-4.I.3:1)

This need not be painful, but it usually is so experienced.
It seems as if things are being taken away,
and it is rarely understood initially that their
lack of value is merely being recognized.

(M-4.I.3:2–3)

I had my own period of undoing a few years ago when I launched my online coaching business and the excitement of being an entrepreneur was soon eclipsed by a response to my first offerings that could charitably be described as lukewarm. This was particularly frustrating because I was working harder than ever and had created products that I was truly proud of, yet nothing was taking off. Around this time I had a conversation with fellow *Course* teacher Gabrielle Bernstein, and as I was telling her about my situation, she gave me some advice I've never forgotten.

"You're making it about you," she said, "and it's not about you."

In that moment I realized that I had spent far too much time and energy focused on *results*—how many units were sold, how many people opened the last email, how many comments were on each post—and I had gradually become disconnected from the *service* aspect of the work itself. Gabby was right. I was making the business about me and missing the larger and more important opportunity to offer value to others. No wonder nothing was happening.

When I started thinking about what I could do differently, I kept returning to a prayer that appears near the beginning of the *Course*:

I am here only to be truly helpful.
I am here to represent Him Who sent me.
I do not have to worry about what to say or what to do,
because He Who sent me will direct me.
I am content to be wherever He wishes,
knowing He goes there with me.
I will be healed as I let Him teach me to heal.

(T-2.V.18:2–6)

By repeating this prayer every day, I discovered that I could instantly shift into a service mode that not only helped with my coaching courses, but it also dissolved my anxiety around other high-pressure projects. For example, I used to be cripplingly nervous when it came to public speaking, but when I got curious about *why*, I realized that this was yet another instance of allowing the lower self to get in the way. Simply put, the *real* pressure was coming from my own fear of being judged: *What if I forget my points? What if my voice shakes? What if I get red-faced and blotchy? What if . . . What if . . . What if . . .*

It is obvious that any situation that causes you concern is associated with feelings of inadequacy, for otherwise you would believe that you could deal with the situation successfully. It is not by trusting yourself that you will gain confidence.

(W-PI.47.5:2–3)

My experiences in both of these very common career scenarios—not seeing the results you desire and becoming fearful in high-pressure situations—are two forms of the same ego cycle. Anxious thoughts were causing me to forget my Magnitude, which in turn caused me to feel alone and judged, which resulted in even more anxiety, and the fear started all over again. Thus, when I found a quiet space to get centered using the above prayer in the moments before going onstage or coaching a client, I was able to defuse ego thinking by recognizing that my function is, first and foremost, simply to extend Love.

When it comes to your own career, in what areas are you "making it about you?" When have you had something happen that seemed devastating at the time, but when you look back you recognize it was actually a gift? How can you incorporate the *Course* prayer above and change your mindset from getting to giving? Whether you answer just one of these questions or all of them, please take a moment to share what comes to you in the space provided.

KEY QUOTES

- The Holy Spirit is the spirit of joy. (T-5.II.2:1)
- For several minutes let your mind be cleared of all the foolish cobwebs which the world would weave around the holy Son of God. (W-pI.139.12:2)
- Practice in earnest, and the gift is yours. (W-pI.164.9:5)
- Forgive and be forgiven. As you give you will receive. There is no plan but this for the salvation of the Son of God. (W-pI.122.6:3-5)

Epilogue

A NEW DEPTH OF BEING

A few years ago I was traveling to Huntington, West Virginia, with a former boss and mentor. Bob was the founder of an accounting firm that had recently been acquired by a much larger company, and while he could have easily retired, he had decided instead to teach undergrads at the university where I was scheduled to present that evening.

When I arrived on campus I was thrilled, though not surprised, when many of the students immediately came up to me praising Bob as "the best professor" they'd ever had and noting how "lucky" I was to have worked with him. I knew what they meant. Bob is one of those rare colleagues who has the ability to push you to your potential in the kindest way possible.

As we were driving home, I happened to notice a plain white CD case peeking out of the console in Bob's car with the word "miracles" handwritten on the front. When I asked what he was listening to, Bob somewhat hesitatingly mentioned that he was listening to "a book called *A Course in Miracles*" on his daily commute.

"I'm familiar with that book," I smiled. "How long have you been a student?"

"Oh, I'm not sure exactly," Bob replied, "but I'd say at least twenty years."

In that moment I knew I had unlocked the secret to Bob's success. I instantly understood why he cared so deeply about the development of others, why he never seemed impatient or flustered, and why he remained so humble despite all he'd achieved.

Bob is the kind of leader I believe the *Course* is calling us to be. He does not wear his faith on his sleeve—to be honest, this was the first time it had come up in ten years of working together—and yet he clearly demonstrates the spiritual Magnitude discussed throughout these pages. Bob, and so many others, are proof that you can indeed honor your interior experience while engaging effectively in the world.

Despite the fact that Western cultures in particular tend to keep these ideas compartmentalized, if you're reading this I'm sure that you also want to live and lead from a spiritual center—and you are not alone. Millions of professionals are looking at the old paradigms of success and wondering what else is possible. They are searching for a deeper layer of meaning and propelled by the most infamous fork-in-the-road question of all: *Is this it?*

Those who have already been introduced to their Magnitude are gently whispering, "*No. There is something else unseen.*" **These are the miracle workers.** They are the ones who look upon an increasingly divisive, wobbly world and point to a better way. Miracle workers are Love's teachers. Like Bob, they don't often announce themselves as what they are, and their voices are not shouting to be heard. But they are around you now, and you'll know them by their frequent smile, quiet eyes, serene forehead, and approach to the world that "is not here, although it seems to be." (W-p1.155.1:1–3)

They come from all over the world. They come from all religions and from no religion. They are the ones who have answered.

(M-1.2:1–3)

By answering the call, miracle workers share what they have learned. They do not force a spiritual discussion, but they do hold space for it because they know only Spirit can transform the heart. Their words teach of Love, and their presence is an invitation to walk in the "lighted footsteps" of forgiveness. (W-p1.134.14:3)

Today, each moment in fact, there is a renewed call for teachers. Listen in your office now and you can hear it. Every turbulent conversation, every impatient exchange, even the most trivial sideways glance carries within it an appeal for Love that is hidden to everyone *except* the miracle workers. They are the ones who have the spiritual vision that enables them to answer these appeals by extending Love while ignoring the fear. Previously, I mentioned that this is a superpower at work—which means that Love's teachers are true superheroes. Indeed, they may not be faster than a speeding bullet, but they have the power to save the world nonetheless.

You have it too, but only if you join Love's messengers by standing in the fullness of your Magnitude and rejecting all littleness. If you're ready, you can start this instant. There are no verses to memorize, no rituals to attend, and no one you need to recruit. All you have to do to accept your role as a miracle worker is to happily bring your own thoughts of separation, judgment, hurt, worry, comparison, attack, and scarcity to the Holy Spirit and allow them to be transformed into forgiveness. Nothing more. You won't need to change careers, and you certainly won't need a cape to rescue yourself or anyone else from the ego. Your presence *is* the alternative.

Can the salvation of the world be a trivial purpose?
And can the world be saved if you are not?

(W-P1.20.3:4–5)

So don't wait until tomorrow to be the joyful, wise, and compassionate leader you are here to be. Accept the call to be a miracle worker now—not just for your own sake, but for the sake of those around you whose own Magnitude has been abandoned for far too long. They will know the Truth about themselves as they see this light in you and in others. And after all the illusions of separation vanish, leaving Love and Love alone, you will know that *this* is your true career.

To your Magnitude,
Emily

How Do I Handle This?

YOUR *MIRACLES AT WORK* QUESTIONS ANSWERED

The following is a selection of questions from *Course* students and coaching clients that I want to share as a way to continue the conversation we've started in this book. As you'll see, some of these questions relate to very specific workplace situations, while others reflect a higher-level approach with a more universal application. I hope you find what you learn here helpful when it comes to practically incorporating *Course* principles into your own career path.

P.S. If you would like to ask a question and connect to our growing community of *Course* students, please visit miraclesatworkbook.com.

Q *How will I know when the* Course *is having the transformative effect on my work and career that I'm looking for?*

You'll know the *Course* is working when you're at peace. In your career, this means a mind that is able to sustain a deep calm regardless of your circumstances or any chaos that surrounds you. This sense of peace will come to you in different ways, but most students have their first *aha* when they begin to observe their ego mind without judging it. You'll also start to notice those moments when you are "getting rid" of your peace by actively keeping conflict going—fanning the flames of annoyance, for example, until they ignite into anger. Over time you'll become less willing to go there, which will only give you more leadership presence and emotional maturity on the job.

In addition, you'll also know the *Course* is having a positive effect when you remember to ask for a holy instant as your bridge back to

Love, resulting in the spiritual vision required to see the Magnitude within yourself and others for extended periods of time. If you ever feel lost in this regard—that is, if you can't find your sense of peace at work—remember this classic career advice: as much as you may love your job, it will never love you back. In other words, it's the *experience* of connection that you're ultimately looking for, and this experience can only occur between *people*. This is why forgiveness is your primary function according to the *Course* and the ripple effect of this practice at work is significant. It's forgiveness that makes *healing your mind* possible, it's a healed mind that makes *true connection* possible, and it's true connection that makes *achievement* possible.

Q: ***Any advice on how to stay composed in a meeting that is getting heated?***

First and foremost, any time you are not at peace is the time to ask for a miracle: *Please help me see this differently. Let me know this brother as I know myself.* Just keep praying your way home until you feel the emotion within you begin to lift and you return to a state of nonjudgment. To be clear, however, note that the ego's judgment is typically condemnation, which is different from judgment in the sense of normal, everyday discernment between ideas or objects.

As such, before you speak up at any point in the meeting, simply ask yourself this one invaluable question: *Will what I'm about to say right now reduce or enhance this person's comfort in communicating openly with me?* You can also phrase the question as: *Will what I'm about to say expand or contract my connection to this person?*

As you may have noticed already, the more miracle-minded you become, the less impulsive you are when you speak; thus, the less likely you are to say something that you'll regret later. Along that line, it's helpful to remember that the moment you can sense the other person escalating their tone, *it's a sign that you're not listening to them at the level they desire to be heard.* If you can get underneath their words to the specific fear that is driving them, then you'll have a much better chance of actually communicating in your meeting, versus wasting everyone's time by talking over each other.

Q ***I'm afraid of communicating from my ego, so sometimes I don't speak up when I feel confronted. How can I stand up for myself at work and be Loving at the same time?***

It's clear that ego thinking can poison your work relationships through attack and blame, but this does not mean the loving response is silence—not at all. Obviously, the higher you go in your career, the more difficult conversations you are likely to have, and if your tendency is to shrink or say nothing, then not only are you dishonoring your own growth, but you are also intercepting the growth of another person.

One tip that may help is to speak only about *your* experience versus making guesses about someone else's motivations or intentions. In other words, it's better to say, "*I'm* feeling some tension here," than it is to say, "*You're* out of control." As another example, let's imagine that you're having a conversation where someone is starting to get aggressive and you're concerned that you could react from your ego at any moment. In these situations, remember that, from a *Course* perspective, Magnitude is your power and defenselessness is its expression. This means your first response—always—is to ask for a miracle that allows you to restore your peace. Next, perhaps you would simply acknowledge your experience: "*When you communicate this way, it's hard for me to connect with what you're saying.*" The point here is that you are not meeting aggression with aggression—meaning your ego is not confronting their ego—but, rather, that you are merely communicating *your* truth as you understand it. As you continue to apply these tools, remember to keep asking for help within your own mind, knowing that (most likely) you will not be guided with specific answers. Instead you will be led to an *experience* of Love that enables you to forgive. As always, go for the *connection* first and trust that the right words will follow.

***Q** How am I supposed to have career goals and yet be in a space of openness and nonattachment at the same time? I get the "pull versus push" mentality, but I just don't know how to apply it at work.*

The idea that success emerges through pulling versus pushing is obviously not a new one (I wrote about this extensively in my book for women leaders), but it does elicit a certain amount of confusion in the workplace, where performance is often measured in metrics. Clearly, companies revolve around goals, and "successful" people are expected to do the same. The problem, of course, is that an overinvestment in the outcome and timing of our goals creates a tremendous amount of anxiety that lodges us deeper and deeper in ego thinking. In our careers, this explains why we routinely compare ourselves to others, why we often don't feel worthy of our dreams, and why so many of us have the nagging feeling that everyone else has things figured out while we're left eating their dust.

As the *Course* says, "A major hazard to success has been involvement with your past and future goals." (W-pI.181.4:1) That said, it's important to remember that when the *Course* uses the word "success," it's not talking about *outward* success. It's talking about success in the form of inner peace and presence that radiates naturally when you resist the ego's delusions. This is the spiritual meaning of pull versus push at work. When you no longer depend on attaining something external to be at peace, your behavior becomes less erratic; hence, other people want to be around you more.

Of course, this does not mean that you're being asked to surrender your goals entirely. It only means that your *first* goal in any situation is to acknowledge the shared light (Magnitude) of a fellow human being. From a *Course* perspective, nothing you could ever achieve or desire is more important than this. Thus, the point here—and this is for *your own* success and happiness—is to shift your focus from *striving* to *service*, where your intention is to simply be a vessel for the presence of Love in each moment, rather than trying to get what you think you need.

In fact, the *Course* repeatedly states our problem is that we *don't know* what we need. We get so caught up in our own goals that we forget, again, that what we're ultimately looking for is connection. Because of this, we often miss things that are not only a better fit for us, but are oftentimes even greater than what we're currently envisioning for ourselves. To put it another way, when you assume that you know what's best, as Rumi said, you are often "hunting for the diamond necklace that is already around your neck."

This point becomes particularly significant at times when you feel unhappy about your career goals because, presumably, you've already tried to figure out everything on your own and it's just not working. So now it's time to try something different. It's time to release the attachment to outcome, goals, and control, and focus on cultivating your miracle mindset instead.

For example, going back to the holy instant, when you look at the distance between where you are and where you want to be, you can simply say, "I need a miracle." Just by taking this one step you automatically become open to something new because what you're essentially saying here is, "I can't trust my own judgment in this situation." This is great news, spiritually speaking, because it is precisely your willingness to surrender your old way of thinking that creates space for the new way. *In other words, you can't effectively ask for help while believing you already know the answer at the same time.* This is why relying on your own judgment is fundamentally incompatible with a holy instant. By attempting to have both control *and* surrender at once you create the kind of confusion in your mind that will only keep you at war with yourself. (As the *Course* says, "If you are trusting in your own strength, you have every reason to be apprehensive, anxious, and fearful." [W-pI.47.1:1])

Accordingly, the solution when it comes to achieving your goals at work is not to *want* but to *become*. This means letting go of your career as yet another idol and replacing questions around what you "need" with a much better one: *Who are you* being *right now?* Show up in full Magnitude *today* and it won't just be possible to build on your success tomorrow—it will be inevitable.

Q ***A very important deal I have been working on just fell through—not my fault!—and I feel frustrated and downhearted. I'm worried that I'm not going to hit my numbers this quarter and this has me in a state of borderline panic. How can I find my way back to peace?***

Again, since every experience begins with a thought, remember that you have the power to change your experience simply by changing your thinking about it. As an example, when you have a thought such as "not my fault," notice the projection there. Something unforeseen happened with negative consequences to your bottom line; however, as long as you consider yourself the "victim" of it, you actually create the reality in which you give away your power. In your case, by viewing yourself as helpless you actually *became* helpless; thus, your thinking created your experience.

From a *Course* perspective, moments like these give you yet another opportunity to listen to your inner guidance. As always, you begin with a simple prayer—for example, *I could see peace instead of this* (W-pI.34)—and as your thoughts shift back from fear to Love, you'll reclaim the power you have to shift your experience. Perhaps you'll make a few more sales calls, or perhaps you'll go visit more prospects; regardless, you won't be sitting around in your office feeling panicked and fearful.

If you're still not sure what "inner guidance" is, remember that the *Course* says we all have the Voice for God (Holy Spirit), a voice for the self (ego), and the power to choose between them. This is not a "special" gift available to a select few; it's available to everyone, although the *Course* does state that your ability to hear it is dependent upon how willing you are to listen. Throughout this and all your challenges, stay focused on what you can control (your thoughts), learn how to listen, act on the guidance you receive, and remember that—no matter what—you are always safe.

Q *I just got into an argument with a client and I know the* **Course** *says that "I'm not my body" so I cannot be attacked. But the truth is, I'm feeling* **extremely** *attacked. How can I apply this lesson at work in a really practical way?*

While the *Course* does say that you cannot be attacked at the level of Spirit, I recognize how unsatisfying this can feel in the moment. As such, I want to be clear that you are not being asked to ignore or rebuff anything regarding how you feel in the body. In fact, one of the misconceptions about looking at the world through a lens of spiritual intelligence (SQ) is that you are somehow being asked to ignore or reject your physical experience, and this is not the case. The *Course* even calls rejecting your body a "particularly unworthy form of denial." (T-2.IV.3:11)

All you are really being asked to deny is the *power* you would give the body to determine your worth and success. For example, in your situation it's clear that you're upset; however, the *Course* would say that you're actually *not* upset because of what your client has or has not *given* you, which in this case I assume would be respect. Rather, the *Course* would say that you're upset because you feel you need respect to *complete* you. If you weren't somehow attached to being given respect, then you wouldn't be upset in the first place.

Therefore, rather than "fight back," your job is to discover what this other person has triggered *in you* that has caused you to forget your Self and feel attacked. Whatever it is, bringing your ego-based thinking to the light gives you the opportunity to address (and ultimately dissolve) it versus keeping it hidden where it will inevitably pop up again in even more attack, defensiveness, and blame.

This is where your spiritual vision comes in because when you have the ability to see beyond the body's behavior, ironically, this is what enables you to behave with more wisdom in the body. Again, when someone else no longer has the power to make you feel weakened, *that's* when you can no longer be attacked because you've no longer granted anyone else permission to write your story.

***Q** I read the paper every morning, and I find that I tend to bring the stress of the world into my job. How can I stay informed without allowing the news to affect my whole day?*

If you pay attention to the news and you learn about something horrific that happened, it's very easy to subconsciously internalize that fear and take it with you to work each day. That said, according to the *Course*, the idea is not to ignore what's happening in the world or to turn away from the suffering of others. Instead, the idea is to elevate the conversation within yourself around it. For example, if you see a story that is upsetting, instead of getting pulled into the negativity of it, notice what's happening and turn it over to your Higher Self, saying, for example, *Please help me see this differently*. As before, the more you practice shifting your perspective in this way, the more you will pull your anxiety from an *unrecognized* place—where it will show up in all forms of self-sabotage anyway—back to a *conscious* place where it can be gently dismissed.

Also, it's important to remember that despite what's happening abroad, across town, or even in your own office, as the saying goes, *vengeance is a lazy form of grief.* In other words, anger in all its forms is an indulgence. Even pity is an indulgence. If left unchecked, they both become reasons to feel powerless that quickly morph into excuses to stay stuck. Yes, when bad things happen it's appropriate to mourn, to be angry, and to feel the way you feel. The issue isn't emotion itself. The issue is *wallowing* in it because wallowing is what creates the ego block that prevents you from moving forward. This applies as much to your career as it does to your morning paper, by the way, because the same principle is true regardless: *If you only see the problems, how could you possibly be available for the solution?*

As such, here's what it boils down to: read the paper and *then go to work and stand for the alternative*. Show through *your* own light and by *your* example that, as one person shifts from anger to action, doors open for others to do the same. Harnessed correctly, this kind of Love *can* transform the world as much as it can transform your business. But, first, you must awaken it in yourself.

About *A Course in Miracles*

FREQUENTLY ASKED QUESTIONS

Q

What is* A Course in Miracles*?

Although *A Course in Miracles* can be unpacked endlessly, it is first and foremost, as the title suggests: a *course*. Within its pages students will find a complete curriculum of spiritual growth and healing that occurs when fear-based thinking is exchanged for holy Love. This shift in perspective is the "miracle" that gives the book its name.

Q

How will this path benefit my career?

With the level of disruption and uncertainty found in business today, leaders must respond to these and other pressures with greater poise, agility, and patience than ever before. While *A Course in Miracles* isn't a spiritual practice designed specifically for careers, the benefit of applying its message *to* your career is that you learn to view your circumstances—regardless of what they may be—from a "miracle-minded" perspective. This enables you to navigate through challenges and personality conflicts with wisdom and compassion rather than allowing yourself to be at the mercy of all that is occurring around you.

How is the material presented?

The formal *Course in Miracles* comprises three parts:

1. The Text: thirty-one chapters that outline the *Course*'s thought system

2. The Workbook: a series of 365 lessons (one for each day of the year) that offer practical ways to apply the principles of the text

3. The Manual for Teachers: a Q&A-style supplement that provides direct answers to twenty-eight common *Course* questions plus a Clarification of Terms

Some copies of the *Course* also come with two supplements that were also scribed by Helen Schucman. These include *Psychotherapy: Purpose, Process and Practice* and *The Song of Prayer: Prayer, Forgiveness, Healing*. The latter is quoted in this book.

Who wrote it?

A Course in Miracles began, as the preface states, with "the sudden decision of two people to join in a common goal." Originally, those two people were Helen Schucman and her colleague William Thetford. As legend has it, for years Helen and Bill—both high-level academics in a pressured, dysfunctional work environment—increasingly found the difficulties of their surroundings boiling over into their personal relationship.

Then, in June of 1965, Bill announced that he'd had enough of the open hostility and endless rounds of heated meetings. In a declaration that was motivated by both passion and exhaustion, Bill said he wanted to find a new method of relating to one another, one that focused on kindness and respect instead of attack and blame.

"There must," he said, "be another way."

Helen, touched by Bill's sincerity, wholeheartedly agreed and committed to help. As *A Course in Miracles* would later describe, this "little willingness" was the only thing needed to create a "holy instant": a moment when all past wounds are dropped and the goal of healing occurs.

Shortly after Helen and Bill agreed to join together in search of a better way to work, Helen began experiencing what she described as a startling series of vivid dreams and strange images. She also began to hear an inner voice, which, on the evening of October 21, 1965, announced, in Helen's words, with "calm but impressive authority" what was to come.

"This is a Course in Miracles. Please take notes."

In the section of the preface called How It Came, Helen described her experience of the Voice as follows:

> It made no sound, but seemed to be giving me a kind of rapid, inner dictation which I took down in a shorthand notebook.

Q What was this "Voice"?

From the opening sentences of the introduction, the *Course* uses second-person language to speak directly to the reader ("Only the time you take it is voluntary"). However, beginning in chapter 1 with miracle principle 27, the text occasionally shifts into first person ("A miracle is a universal blessing from God through me"). This back-and-forth continues throughout the writing, but it's especially jarring at the beginning because you're probably wondering, *Okay, who's talking here?*

According to Helen, the Voice she heard—and therefore the author of *A Course in Miracles*—is Jesus.

Since we have no way to validate Helen's experience, as you continue your *Course* journey you'll just have to decide for yourself:

Is this the work of an imaginative psychologist, or is it a bona fide celestial breakthrough?

Whatever your personal opinions are related to how the book came into being, one thing is true regardless: belief that Jesus was the author of the *Course* is not required in order to benefit from the wisdom within its pages.

Q *Who was Jesus in the* Course?

Since the birth of Christianity, Jesus has been viewed as God's only son, implying that he has achieved a divine position that we could never share. The message of the *Course* is that Jesus is God's son, yes, but no more or less than you. From a *Course* perspective, the true legacy of Jesus is that he "was the first to complete his own part perfectly" (C-6.2:2), meaning he walked the earth in a state of oneness with God—entirely free from the perception of separation—and, thus, he demonstrated it could be done. The *Course* does not claim that Jesus has been or will be the only person to do this; however, it *does* claim that he can be called upon to free you from your own limiting perceptions at your request. In this sense, Jesus is an "elder brother" (T-1.II.4:5) whose role is to help you "bridge the distance" (T-1.II.4:5) back to God, a gap that would otherwise be "too great for you to encompass." (T-1.II.4:4).

Q *How does the* Course *relate to other spiritual paths? Is it Christian?*

The preface to the *Course* states it is "but one version of the universal curriculum" that "all lead to God in the end." In other words, every great spiritual path has awakening to holy Love at its center and the *Course* is no different in this regard. As to whether the *Course* is Christian, the preface goes on to describe it as "Christian in statement" but dealing with "universal spiritual themes." This means that, while Christians may recognize the *language* used in the *Course*, the *message* is universal and transcends any and all religious ties. As such, the answer to this question is: yes and no. *Yes* in the sense that there are more than eight hundred direct quotations or references to Biblical passages in the *Course*, not to mention Jesus as the stated narrator. But *no* because there are some key distinctions between *Course* philosophy and traditional Christianity, which we have explored throughout this book.

For students coming from Eastern traditions, the nondualistic tenets of the *Course* (explained here in chapter 1) will no doubt sound very familiar. In fact, the *Course* has occasionally been described as a "Christian Vedanta" due to its alignment with segments of Hindu philosophy, and certainly anyone wishing to dig deeper will find overlaps with other paths as well. Accordingly, it is fair to wonder whether the *Course* is merely a collection of ancient spiritual principles neatly packaged for modern-day seekers. While I can't credibly defend the *Course*'s assertion of being divinely channeled (I wasn't there, after all), what I can say is that, based on the writings of those who knew her, Helen did not appear to be a student of any religion other than Christianity—and she had a very love/hate relationship with her own beliefs around that.

Q *I can't deal with the word "God." Is the* Course *for me?*

Certainly the concept of God conjures up different associations with different people and not all of them are positive. That said, one thing I've learned along my own spiritual journey is this: the less you try to label what it is you're looking for—and *definitely* the less you try to label what every else should be looking for—the better you will be able to find it. We each have a "God" of our own understanding, so if you prefer not to use this language to describe what that means to you, no problem. Sometimes when I'm reading the *Course* I'll replace the word "God" with "love," "wisdom," or "compassion" and you're welcome to do the same—or you're welcome to make up a new term altogether if you prefer. As it says in the *Course*, words are but symbols anyway. It's the meaning we give them that counts.

Q *Why does the* Course *use masculine pronouns?*

It's true that the *Course* uses only masculine terms—calling God "He," referencing the "Sons of God," "brothers," and the like—and it's understandable that this would raise eyebrows and alarm bells in students who are concerned about the not-so-subtle messaging this language could send about power, influence, and hierarchy. (You're reading this from a woman who wrote a career book called *Who Says It's a Man's World*, so believe me, I get it.) This is why I want to state clearly that the *Course* has zero interest in gender. The *Course* is about spiritual growth *and spirit has no gender*. Moreover, it's a flawed aspect of the English language that there isn't a word that encapsulates both "he" and "she" into one grammatically correct pronoun. However, this is our issue, not the *Course*'s. If the patriarchal language is a distraction, again, feel free to substitute any words that feel right to you. Or better yet, as the *Course* reminds us, forget the words altogether and *go for the experience*.

Q *Are there multiple versions of the* Course?

When *A Course in Miracles* was first published in 1976, readers assumed that the material presented was in complete form and exactly as Helen Schucman heard it. Then, in 2000, an earlier manuscript appeared on the web, quickly followed by the urtext, the original draft Bill typed directly from Helen's notes. Consequently, there is ongoing confusion and debate in *Course* circles about which text represents the "authentic" material.

Therefore, the short answer is *yes*, there are different versions of the *Course*, though it's important to note that the vast majority of edits fall within the first four chapters only. In the earliest drafts, those chapters appear more as a conversation between Helen and the Voice, a conversation later deemed full of errors and discrepancies resulting from Helen's fear of the process. In any event, many *Course* students have their favorite version but, true to the *Course* itself, at the end of the day what matters most isn't the form of the book but the content of the message, which remains unchanged in them all.

The "Original Four" Who Brought Us *A Course in Miracles*

Scribe: Helen Schucman (1909–1981), clinical psychologist and professor at Columbia University's College of Physicians and Surgeons in New York City. Helen wrote *A Course in Miracles* in a series of notebooks from an "inner dictation" she identified as Jesus. After scribing and editing the material, Helen rarely spoke publicly about her connection to the *Course*, and even at her funeral, her role in its birth was never mentioned.

Co-scribe: William Thetford (1923–1988), professor at Columbia University's College of Physicians and Surgeons and director of clinical psychology at Columbia–Presbyterian Hospital, now New York–Presbyterian Hospital. Bill was the first person Helen confided in when she began the dictation that would become *A Course in Miracles*. Originally, Bill offered to type Helen's notes as a gesture to help with her anxiety about "hearing a voice," but as the book's depth and sophistication unfolded, Bill continued this role for seven years, from 1965 until 1972. Once the initial manuscript was complete, Bill, who did not experience the same inner Voice as Helen, quietly remained a student of the *Course* until his death in 1988.

Editor: Kenneth Wapnick, PhD (1942–2013), clinical psychologist and the first teacher of *A Course in Miracles*. Ken was introduced to Helen and Bill in the fall of 1972 following completion of the original manuscript (urtext). Upon reading the material, Ken, who was planning to become a monk, decided not to enter the monastery and instead worked closely with Helen to edit and prepare the *Course* for publication. Ken went on to become a prolific spiritual teacher and scholar, authoring thirty-four books on the *Course* during his lifetime.

Publisher: Judith Skutch Whitson (b. 1933), experimental psychology professor at New York University and executive director of the Foundation for Inner Peace. Judy received a copy of the *Course* from

Helen and Bill in the spring of 1975. Enchanted with the book's insight, Judy organized the first-edition release of the *Course* a year later and has been actively involved with the publication ever since.

ACKNOWLEDGMENTS

Heartfelt thanks . . .

To my agent, Linda Konner. I know this book was as much of a surprise to you as it was to me, and your continued support and counsel are deeply appreciated.

To my Sounds True family—Jennifer Brown, Haven Iverson, Sarah Gorecki, and Tami Simon—for believing in this project and giving me the opportunity to bring it to life. I also want to thank Jennifer Holder for championing *Miracles at Work* from the very beginning and Sheridan McCarthy for beautifully seeing it through to the finish.

To my mentors Kenneth Wapnick and Marianne Williamson, whose eloquence, scholarship, and prolific teachings have unlocked the *Course* for me and so many others. If you feel this book has enhanced your own understanding of the *Course*, I give much of the credit to these teachers and their extraordinary library of resources. Marianne, you are my hero, and it is a true honor to have your beautiful words as the Foreword to this book. From the bottom of my heart, thank you.

To Robert Perry for your remarkable and unwavering commitment to the integrity of the *Course*, and for generously providing early feedback that greatly benefited these pages.

To Judith Skutch Whitson, the Foundation for Inner Peace, the Foundation for *A Course in Miracles*, Pathways of Light, Miracle Distribution Center, Jon Mundy, Beverly Hutchinson McNeff, and Carol Howe for being such committed and inspiring lamp carriers for students of the *Course*.

To Gabrielle Bernstein for being the first to introduce me to the *Course* on, naturally, 3.11.11. It was your bright light that revealed this path and for that I will always be grateful.

To Viktor Frankl, Stephen Covey, and Mel Robbins for showing me "the space" between stimulus and response.

To the Abbey of Gethsemani and Mepkin Abbey monks for opening your sacred doors, inspiring me with your discipline, and providing a quiet space for this writing.

To my parents, Paul Bennington and Lynn Cook, for the many lessons you've taught me in this life.

To Johnny, Christian, and Liam Tugwell. No words are enough to express what a joy and privilege it is to be on this ever-winding path with you.

Finally, to the miracle workers who are committed to bringing the light, standing for the alternative, and sharing your Magnitude each and every day. I bow to you all.

NOTES

Introduction: Is Business Spiritual?

1. Pew Research Center Religion and Public Life, *The Global Religious Landscape Survey*, pewforum.org/2012/12/18/global-religious-landscape-exec/, 2012.

2. Bureau of Labor Statistics, *American Time Use Survey*, bls.gov/tus/charts/home.htm, 2014.

Chapter 1

1. Cindy Wigglesworth, *SQ21: The Twenty-One Skills of Spiritual Intelligence* (New York: SelectBooks, 2014), 8.

Chapter 2

1. Most spiritual intelligence (SQ) programs developed specifically to be taught in a business setting do not discuss belief *by design* in an effort to avoid religious debate. Please see chapter 7 for more on this topic.

Chapter 7

1. Wigglesworth, *SQ21: The Twenty-One Skills of Spiritual Intelligence*, 8.

Chapter 8

1. Adapted from *A Course in Miracles* (T-2.VI).

ABOUT THE AUTHOR

Emily Bennington is a bestselling author and a student / teacher of contemplative practices for both secular and spiritual audiences. She has led training programs on composure and values-driven leadership for numerous Fortune 500 companies and has been featured in press ranging from CNN, ABC, and Fox, to the *Wall Street Journal*, *Glamour*, *Marie Claire*, and *Cosmopolitan*.

In addition to *Miracles at Work*, Emily is the author of two other books: *Effective Immediately: How To Fit In, Stand Out, and Move Up at Your First Real Job* and *Who Says It's a Man's World: The Girls' Guide to Corporate Domination*, which was featured as a "Book of the Month" by the *Washington Post*. As a result of her business background, Emily is skilled at presenting complex mindfulness and spiritual topics with logical reasoning, professionalism, and inclusiveness. While her work is gender neutral, Emily's website was recently listed by *Forbes* as one of the "100 Best" for women, and her blog, Grace, touches thousands of readers around the world who are seeking to live and lead with more holistic presence and joy. For more information, an events schedule, and online course offerings, please visit emilybennington.com.

For companion bonuses related to this book, please visit miraclesatworkbook.com.

ABOUT SOUNDS TRUE

Sounds True is a multimedia publisher whose mission is to inspire and support personal transformation and spiritual awakening. Founded in 1985 and located in Boulder, Colorado, we work with many of the leading spiritual teachers, thinkers, healers, and visionary artists of our time. We strive with every title to preserve the essential "living wisdom" of the author or artist. It is our goal to create products that not only provide information to a reader or listener, but that also embody the quality of a wisdom transmission.

For those seeking genuine transformation, Sounds True is your trusted partner. At SoundsTrue.com you will find a wealth of free resources to support your journey, including exclusive weekly audio interviews, free downloads, interactive learning tools, and other special savings on all our titles.

To learn more, please visit SoundsTrue.com/freegifts or call us toll-free at 800.333.9185.